WRITE IN STYLE

HOW TO USE YOUR COMPUTER TO IMPROVE YOUR WRITING

D1594054

ALSO BY BOBBIE CHRISTMAS

NONFICTION

Write In Style: Using Your Word Processor and Other Techniques to Improve Your Writing (2004)

Purge Your Prose of Problems: A Book Doctor's Desk Reference (Five editions from 1998 – 2011)

Ask the Book Doctor: How to Beat the Competition and Sell You. Writing (2005)

FICTION

The Legend of Codfish and Potatoes with coauthor Dale Butler, M.P. (1999)

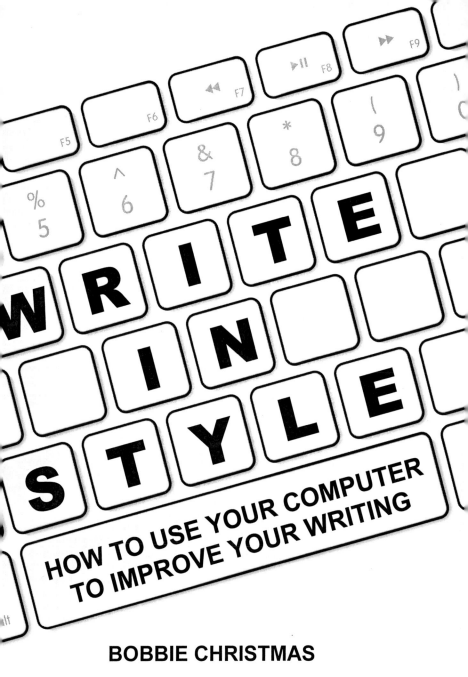

WRITE IN STYLE

HOW TO USE YOUR COMPUTER TO IMPROVE YOUR WRITING

BOBBIE CHRISTMAS

2ND EDITION

**BOOK**LOGIX®

Alpharetta, GA

Copyright © 2015 by Bobbie Christmas

All rights reserved. No part of this book may be reproduced or transmitted in any form or by any means, electronic or mechanical, including photocopying, recording, or any information storage and retrieval system, without permission in writing from the publisher. For more information, address BookLogix, c/o Permissions Department, 1264 Old Alpharetta Rd., Alpharetta, GA 30005.

ISBN: 978-1-61005-663-2

2nd Edition

10 9 8 7 6 5 4 3 2   0 6 0 9 1 5

Printed in the United States of America

♾This paper meets the requirements of ANSI/NISO Z39.48-1992 (Permanence of Paper)

CONTENTS

INTRODUCTION

Other books teach grammar; this ain't one of 'em. This book assumes you know the basics and are ready to produce memorable literature, persuasive proposals, alluring ad copy, and other creative writing.

I will show you how to step away from your work and view it with an objective eye. Along with dozens of tips, you will learn my Find and Refine Method™, a system I devised for Microsoft Word to speed you through your final manuscript tune-up. *Write In Style* teaches you how to create your own crisp, clean style, so everything you write gets even better. When you apply the principles in this book, you produce enticing articles, marketable books, scintillating short stories, credible copy, potent proposals, and intelligible manuals.

Why is Style a Big Deal?

Smart writers create a crisp writing style that produces tight, polished manuscripts that pull ahead of the pack and sell more often. Only a few writers take the time to learn about style, and you are one of the shrewd few, because I am about to make you a smart writer.

I speak often about winning, and a ragged-running manuscript—one you have not tuned up, polished, and written in style—gets rejected. It loses. Period. No writer wants rejection in any form, whether writing books, sales letters, short stories, proposals, advertisements, sermons, essays, or anything else.

If style makes the difference, why don't all writers improve their style and win whatever their hearts desire? Simple. Style is subjective. Few people have the capacity to evaluate their own writing. Some authors who work hard to create their own style turn out purple prose, rather than powerful prose. Up to now, no objective method existed to point out weak writing, overwritten prose, or what I call "missed opportunities for improvement."

The Secret to Style

I am about to reveal the secret of style, whether it refers to writing or clothes. Too much embellishment and a person changes from classy to gaudy. For example, a pair of pearl earrings and a tidy necklace look classy, but chandelier-sized earrings and a garish necklace with a bedazzled blouse adorned with a huge broach would make any woman look gaudy. The same holds true for writing. When you write in style, you remove embellishments and leave the sleek, appealing essence.

Style applies more often to what you take out of your writing than what you put in.

I will show you what to take out, so you can write in style. The difference will amaze you and work in your favor, no matter what type of writing you do.

One Step at a Time

Do not apply the steps in this book until after you have completed your first or second draft. Rely on your creative side first. Put aside the teachings in this book and get the words down—let your mind, body, and manuscript zoom along as well as you can. Build a solid concept with good structure. Create a compelling story or a complete composition. Stay in your chair until you write from beginning to end. Don't worry about details or writing in style on the first draft or two.

Your best ideas come out in a stream of consciousness, a flow you should not interrupt. I cannot emphasize it enough: first write your book, article, proposal, brochure, training manual, or memo. Some people call it a mind dump.

After you have written the draft, the manuscript will have the content you want, and you and your manuscript will be ready for the information in this book. I'm about to fill your toolbox with great devices that help you clean up, tune up, and complete your project in style. When you follow the tips in this manual, you'll produce friction-free fiction, well-oiled nonfiction, and other marketable prose.

Write In Style makes the lack of style easy to spot and simple to improve. I impart advice and show you how to improve your style using the software program you probably already have installed on your computer. Microsoft Word is the program that has become the standard in the book-publishing industry, but all similar programs have the functions I discuss in this book. You won't have to buy or learn new software. You will use to your advantage the software you already have. You will learn to find key words that point out opportunities to write more creatively.

Join me while I share tips on what editors seek, the elements that persuade publishers to issue a contract, and the type of writing that readers enjoy. I concentrate on standard stylistic methods and teach you how to use advanced technology—the Find and Refine Method—to find your missed opportunities and learn to write in style.

A Little Laughter Lightens the Load

To ensure you understand every tip, I include examples and exercises. In addition, some chapters incorporate outtakes from actual unedited manuscripts. I use those mistakes, which I call Manu-slips, to illustrate points and give you a chuckle. I've changed the characters' names, to protect the writers and their properties.

None of us can escape mistakes. I'm no exception. An in-flight magazine once assigned me an article about a charity golf tournament. I included a sidebar about the recipient of the proceeds, a cancer research center that originally opened as a tuberculosis clinic. I did my research, conducted interviews, wrote the article, read it for errors, fixed all I found, and turned in the finished product.

The editor of the magazine called me in a fit of laughter. He could barely catch his breath. He finally sputtered, "Did you read the opening sentence of your sidebar?"

Indignant, I answered, "Of course."

He guffawed. "I think not. You'd better read it again."

I opened the file on my computer. The first line began, "Many things have changed at The City of Hope since the first few tuberculosis patients set up tents outside San Francisco to seek refuse from the crowds."

"Refuse?" I gasped. "Oh, I meant refuge."

We all make blunders, and we must laugh, learn, and move on.

Are you ready to take your journey and find out how to write in style? Let's get going. It's easier than you think.

WRITE IN STYLE, AND YOU WRITE FOR SUCCESS

Take a moment to consider your reasons for writing. What constitutes success for you? Do you want to see your byline in print, put your feelings on paper, record your personal or family history, or make money?

Every person who applies words to paper has a personal definition of success. On the following page is a list of reasons why some people write. Do you see your reasons on that list?

Study the list and consider how many of the listed reasons for writing apply to you. Close this book for a moment and think about what *winning* means to you. Define your concept of success. Write down your definitions of success, what you would like to happen as a result of writing.

Reopen this book and fill in the blanks with all your reasons for writing, all the ways you wish to achieve success.

I write because I want to do the following things:

1. _____
2. _____
3. _____
4. _____
5. _____

Once you have recorded your motives, copy them and keep the list in full view near your computer or your notepad, wherever you sit and write.

Type of writer	Possible definitions of success
Creative writer	Sell short stories
Novelist	Get novels published
Educational	Writer sell reference books to
Speaker	Offer books at speaking engagements, add a passive income stream, get booked to speak more often
Business writer	Win new customers
Memoir writer	Entertain generations, record family history
Consultant	Build credentials, gain clients, increase cash flow
Proposal writer	Win lucrative contracts
Hobbyist	Win writing competitions
Journalists/freelancers	Win juicy article assignments
Essayists/op-ed writers	Express personal opinions, win converts
Members of the clergy	Earn respect and attention of congregation
Many writers	Earn extra money—or even a living—with words

Why Record Your Reasons for Writing?

Your incentives for writing are also your goals, and you must know your goals, before you can achieve them. Without defined intentions, you lack direction. If you don't know your goals, how will you know if you reach them?

In my seminars, I challenge people to ponder their reasons for writing. I give them a sheet on which to write the answers. When they finish, I congratulate them, because they have set goals, and the first step toward achieving a goal is to write it down. Yes, setting a goal is that simple.

Does such a technique work? You bet it does. I cannot recall who performed the original study of business-school graduates, but the study showed that a few years after students graduated, some had accomplished many things and were earning high incomes, while others saw almost no difference in their careers after they completed the business course. The study discovered that the only difference between the two groups was that the achieving group had written down goals and kept them handy. The group of graduates who had seen little success had no written goals.

My stepbrother Jim read about the study and tested the theory. In his late twenties, he listed the amount of income he wanted to make each year for the next five years and slipped the information into his wallet. Every morning before he left for work, he pulled out the paper and read the dollar amount he wanted to achieve that year. Sure enough, at the end of the first year, he had met his goal. He set aggressive goals for the following years, almost doubling his income every twelve months, yet he met every goal for the next five years. Today he's a successful, wealthy man.

My motto is "A goal is nothing but a dream with a deadline." I have read controversy over who said the quote first, Napoleon Hill or Diana Scharf Hunt, but I do know this: when I write down a goal and set a deadline to meet that goal, I meet it.

After you know what you want, decide when you want it to happen. Fill in a deadline for each of your goals. Your list of goals may look like this:

I write because I want to do the following things:

1. Sell my first novel by my fortieth birthday.
2. Win a Pulitzer by the time I retire.
3. Earn extra income starting with the New Year.
4. See one of my stories in (fill in the name of a publication) by (fill in a date).
5. Have a book I can give away at seminars, so I get booked to speak more often, starting (fill in a date).

Once you have written your goals and added deadlines, look at your written goals often, to engrave the information on your brain. The fact that you wrote down your goals and set deadlines starts you on your path to success.

In case you find such "new-age thought" too bizarre for you, consider that Greek philosopher Aristotle, who was also a scientist, recommended the same techniques 2,400 years ago. He said that to ensure success, a person had to "start with the end in mind." Do the same, and you reach the end you have in mind.

The Find and Refine Method

No matter how you define success, winning at the writing game requires time and creativity. When you apply my Find and Refine Method, you let your computer find "missed opportunities for improvement," so you can revise every sentence to be as powerful as it can be. You supply the time, and the Find and Refine Method improves your creativity.

Writing anything is an investment in time, energy, and sometimes money. To get a return on your investment; to win a publishing contract, a new client, a writing contest, the respect of others; or to win in whatever way you define success, you must write in style. To write in style, you must find the areas that would benefit from improvement, and I will show you how, with the Find and Refine Method.

My Personal Discovery

When I was eighteen or nineteen, I made a mind-boggling discovery. Until that time, I thought I liked to write. In high school I had written and edited newsletters for two clubs. One was a social and civic club and the other, the Spanish Honor Club, required writing and editing in Spanish. I thought I enjoyed the entire process. I got a kick out of seeing the newsletters come off the press filled with the words I had written.

Somewhere around 1965, as I smiled at my byline in a college newspaper, I thought over all I had gone through to get the story. I had formulated the idea, pitched it to the editor, earned the assignment, tracked down the people I needed to interview, conducted the interviews, read and reread my notes, written the article, revised it, retyped it, and turned it in. The editor scanned my article, looked up, and said, "We don't have much room.

Cut it by three inches." I labored over the deletions and revised the article again.

I didn't mind all those steps in the submission process, but I didn't like them, either. At times I wondered if I liked to write at all. As I stared at the byline of the finished article, though, I forgot all the trouble that led to it. At that instant, I understood I did not like to write; I loved having written. I treasured seeing my name in print. The byline made all my efforts worthwhile. Most women don't love pregnancy, but they adore their children. I felt the same about my articles: the incubation and labor were worth the result. Seeing my words in print represented success to me.

If I had aborted the writing process at any point along the way, I would not have seen my name in print. If I had not come up with an original idea, or had I botched the interview or refused to cut the length, I would have lost everything. I did all the work for the final reward, the byline, which made the work worth the trouble. I invested thoughts, energy, time, and paper to bring about the win: my name in print. Today if anybody says to me, "I love to write," I know they probably mean, "I love having written."

Tedious Tasks

Believe me; I know how much work goes into a book, report, manual, article, story, or proposal. After a few drafts, we get tired of the process and want to turn in the finished product. Is it finished, though? Possibly not, and hurrying to turn in an unpolished manuscript is as foolish as driving in a road rally, only to stop half a mile from the finish line. You won't win, no matter how much time and energy you put into the process.

You must remember your goal. You must cross that finish line. You must win. You must succeed in whatever ways you define success, or you have wasted your time. Unpolished manuscripts get ignored, no matter how much time you have put into them. Why would any writer quit without taking the manuscript to the finish line, without giving it enough power to succeed?

Switch Sides

I've been told that the activity of writing draws from our creative senses, the right side of our brain, whereas the editing part draws from the linear-thinking left side of our brain. That's why after writing the first draft, writers must shift from the creative side of the brain to the revising side, and this book shows you how. After you write your manuscript, take off your creative glasses and put on your editing glasses for a final scrutiny with the eye of an editor.

With a final tune-up using an eye for style, you have a greater chance of succeeding, whether success to you means selling your book, story, article, or essay; pleasing a boss; convincing a client; entertaining your family; or something else.

Objective Observation

No matter the level of editing or polishing, writers can never fully correct their own work. First of all, they do not know what they do not know. If they are unaware of the difference between words such as *scraping* and *scrapping*, *comprise* and *compose*, *immigrate* and *emigrate*, or *ensure* and *insure*, for example, they will continue to make the same mistakes.

Writers also grow too close to their prose to see every flaw. They know what they meant to say and think their sentences convey their intent, but only another reader can determine if the meaning is clear. Writers can read their own work a dozen times or three hundred times and still not spot all the defects. Why? They become too intimate with the work. They know what it says, or they think they do. Their eyes skip over material they have read before. Writers no longer see the details in their own work.

To make matters worse, almost all of us have little quirks from our background, things we think are correct or understandable, but they are not. Even educated people may write something like this: "I use to love perfume." The correct form is "I used to love perfume." The mistake is easy; we all say *use to* when we speak.

Another common error I see in manuscripts I edit involves pronouns that refer to the wrong word, sometimes in a way that causes me to laugh. The writers knew which word those pronouns were supposed to modify, so they skip over the error that only an editor can spot. For example, *Sam handed Jim the reins, and they took off at a slow pace.* The writer meant that Sam and Jim took off at a slow pace, but in truth, the pronoun *they* refers to the reins, which seemed to take off by themselves, as written.

If you think something was right when you wrote it, you won't know it's wrong when you attempt to edit your own work.

Although I give you inside secrets and tips for writing with style and show you how to use your computer to allow you to be more objective, I trust you will still find someone reliable to read your work and spot the technical errors you could no longer see. I use the computer techniques in this book, yet I also rely on other readers and editors.

Even more difficult for writers to spot are the missed opportunities to write stronger prose. For example, as a young writer,

I found nothing wrong with the following sentence: *There are some things that my dog hates to do.* In truth, the sentence breaks no rules of grammar or punctuation, so what's the problem? The problem is style. The sentence grows in strength when written this way: *My dog abhors the bath and refuses to sleep in her own bed.* The second sentence gives specifics and avoids wordiness and weak verbs.

You can Succeed When You Want To Succeed

While most writers cannot write well without feedback from colleagues or an editor, you can strengthen your writing, write in style, increase the power of your manuscript, and improve your chances for success by employing the Find and Refine Method.

As with revving up your car, revving up a manuscript requires a combination of operations, rather than one procedure. I can't teach you all the procedures—everything about creative writing—in one book, but I can give you techniques that increase your chances of success. If you strengthen your writing and it still meets with rejection after rejection, you may then choose to hire a professional editor to evaluate the manuscript and edit it from concept to commas.

Slip Into These Shoes

To figure out why you should go to all the trouble of applying the Find and Refine Method and writing in style, put yourself in the buyer's shoes.

When you write a wimpy sales letter, it has no power of persuasion. Receivers easily dump it into the trash bin. The same holds true for a weak book proposal or a sloppily written novel.

Publishers have high standards. If you write a novel, you may want to find an agent to represent it to a major publisher. Legitimate agents accept only the top manuscripts, the cream of the crop, because they cannot waste time with any that are not ready to market.

Publishers also want to get the best value for their investment, and their investment is high. They pay the author, the printer, the publicist, the distributor, the acquisitions manager, and a staff of others. They pay for rent, utilities, and upkeep of their offices and equipment. If publishers spent money on manuscripts that could not return a profit, they would soon be out of business.

Here's the rub: agents and publishers have the training and experience to know what will sell in today's market. In the same vein, other buyers or receivers of proposals, reports, or other writing slough off colorless materials.

Sad to say, few people ever explain what constitutes weak writing. Agents and others in the publishing industry don't have the time to give comments and advice. Potential buyers of your book won't tell you why it didn't grab their interest; they may not even know the answer. Listeners rarely tell speakers, "I thought your speech could have been a little stronger today if you had used more persuasive verbs." You may never know why you didn't succeed, which can be frustrating for any writer.

Manuscripts fail most often because they suffer from wordiness or lack of style. Writers have run most of the rally, but because of bumbling style, their manuscript did not stand a chance against more polished ones. As a writer you expect to win with your writing, but instead, others see the blemishes you cannot see. The result is failure.

The Deceleration Dilemma

You're left with few options. You can trash the manuscript, but you've then wasted your investment in time, paper, hardware, and software. You can try to figure out for yourself what you've done wrong, but you've already tried, and it didn't work. You're too close to your work to see its quirks and oddities. You can pay a book doctor like me to inspect all the internal workings of the manuscript, repair blatant errors, and report further improvements you could undertake to make your manuscript marketable. None of those options may appeal to you, though. Two of them require even more time or money.

Rough versus Stylish Writing

This book gives you the tools you need to find jerky prose and smooth it with style. As you find and address all the opportunities for improvement in your manuscript, you increase your chances of getting a return on your investment. You better your chances of success.

Every example of weak writing in this book creeps into published articles, books, and proposals, yet every item I address represents a missed opportunity to write stronger prose. After you have worked with the principles in this book, you'll also spot missed opportunities in everyone else's writing. Your skills will continue to grow every time you sit at your keyboard or take pen in hand.

This book shows you how to locate and repair the small impurities in your prose. With a few tweaks, turns, and twists, prose changes from mediocre to sparkling, from ragged to smooth, and from weak to powerful. Those who write with style succeed more often and make a mark on the world.

When we first learn to write, we concentrate on grammar. We learn the parts of speech and how each one works. We understand the difference between a noun, a verb, an adverb, and an adjective, and we gain the knowledge of how to put them together to form complete sentences. If we have an interest in writing, we move on to find out how to make our sentences more creative—that is, how to improve our writing style. Creative style makes the difference between pedantic writing and memorable prose. I want to make you a pro with prose. If you learn what the professionals spot as weak writing, you'll know how to write in style. You are about to discover how to put your writing a step ahead of ninety percent of what gets sent to publishers and agents. Peek inside the mind of an independent book editor— often called a book doctor—and glean the knowledge of how to polish your prose to a high shine that gets attention, not by its flamboyance, but by its subtleties, by its smooth flow and unobtrusive style.

After you read and apply my instructions, if you think you still cannot perform the final tweaking of your manuscript, go ahead and hire a professional. Be careful to choose an editor with a good reputation. Ask for references, and check them. Investigate editing companies through the Better Business Bureau, as well.

If you rewrite your piece using the advice in this book and it still collects rejection slips, It could mean you need more help with the content or concept. It could mean you still need the help of an editor. It could also mean you haven't yet reached the right person or right market. Keep trying, keep improving, keep getting feedback, and never give up.

2

TINKER WITH STYLE

Many authors get confused when they hear about style, because the word has several meanings. Style can refer to creative-writing style, as this book does, which applies to word choice and sentence arrangement, the little tweaks and twists that improve the quality of a sentence, paragraph, chapter, and book. Style also can refer to manuscript style, though, so let me explain more clearly, before we return to creative style.

Manuscript Style

Imagine a bank of hundreds of writers, all submitting articles to one service that approves them and sends them to dozens of newspapers, as happens with services such as The Associated Press. Every writer in the pool has gone to a different school, and each school teaches its own set of standards regarding when to capitalize words, where to use commas, how and when to abbreviate words, when to write out a number and when to use numerals, and even when to set words in italics. Imagine the chaos created for the poor editors who have to bring all the articles into one consistent standard.

Grammar rules may be carved in granite, but the rules for punctuation, abbreviation, and capitalization are not. Some teachers instruct their students to put a comma before *and* in a series, as in this sentence: *Joe, Mary, and Paul took a bus to the library.* My high school English teacher taught me to put it in, to avoid an unnatural link between elements. Leaving it out, she taught me, implied that Mary and Paul were more closely related than Joe and Mary. My college professors, however, said to leave out the comma before *and* in a series. They said contemporary style spurned unnecessary commas. Who was right? Where were the rules?

To my surprise, rules are not always rules. To resolve the issue, news agencies and book publishers created guidelines—style books—that addressed variables in punctuation, capitalization, use of numerals, and abbreviation. Each agency created its own style book for its writers to follow, so all articles submitted to and by that news agency would have consistent punctuation, capitalization, use of numerals, and other details, right down to the correct use of titles for dignitaries.

I'm not sure of the order in which the agencies produced their stylebooks, so I don't know which one came first, but over the years, *The Associated Press Stylebook* emerged as the one of choice for many periodicals. Most newspapers and magazines follow Associated Press style, often referred to as AP style. Some create their own variation of it.

Periodicals, however, differ from books, which differ from academic writing, which differs from business writing, although for the life of me, I don't understand why we have so many different styles. Most book publishers bring conformity to book publication through adherence to a style the University of Chicago Press standardized. Chicago style contradicts AP style, at times, yet both are right—for their intended market.

Legal documents and business writing have yet another style. No wonder everyone in your critique circle has a differing opinion about where to put those darned commas and whether and when to capitalize words such as pope, governor, and even president.

Do you need to learn all the differences in manuscript styles? Yes and no. Yes, if you want to sell more work to periodicals. No, possibly, if you're writing books.

All electronic periodicals as well as today's printed magazines and newspapers want articles to arrive electronically needing little editing and no retyping. If you want to sell articles, you would do well to learn each publication's style and follow it to the letter. You'll please your editor, and as a result, get more assignments. I found AP style easy to learn. You can pick up the small *AP Stylebook* in almost any bookstore, and its well-organized format makes finding answers easy.

The Chicago Manual of Style, preferred by book publishers, is another issue entirely. It's a whopping 1,000-plus-page reference book with a stiff retail price, and it has more information than any novelist or nonfiction writer needs. No publisher on earth can expect you to know everything in that book, unless you are an editor. In my decades of working with Chicago style as a book editor, I've committed much of the information to memory, but even I have to look up something now and then.

Publishers can repair small style flaws in a manuscript easily, though. If you submit a well-written, irresistible book, article, or story to the right source, a smart editor will snap it up regardless of whether it follows that publisher's style. If you write average prose, but it conforms to the style of that publication, an editor might buy it instead of some other submission that requires rewriting. When you follow the correct manuscript style, you increase your chances of sales. I don't advocate that you spend months learning all the finite details of Chicago style, though. Trust an editor instead or go to http://zebraeditor.com/free_ reports.shtml and get my free reports #105 and #118, to learn some of the major points of Chicago style.

If you'd still like to become an expert yourself and make sure your book complies with Chicago style, buy *The Chicago Manual of Style*, borrow a copy, or subscribe to *The Chicago Manual of Style* online, to bring your book into compliance. If you decide instead to hire an editor, don't hire just any editor, but choose a book editor familiar with Chicago style, to bring your book up to par.

More people than ever have computers and are writing. Because of the volume of submissions that publishers and agents receive, you must do whatever you can to get your manuscript as ready for publication as possible before you submit it. Using correct manuscript style helps put your manuscript at least one notch ahead of others.

Creative Style

For the remainder of this book, when I speak of style I won't mean manuscript style—when and where to punctuate, capitalize, abbreviate, or spell out something. Instead the rest of this book refers to creative style, which occurs at the word level. I can't wait to show you the miraculous changes you can make in your manuscript, simply through your choice of words. Let's go right to chapter three, where I discuss pronouns and how they affect the quality of your writing.

Some of the future chapters include creative-writing exercises. I encourage you to take a few minutes to type in the exercises and revise and rewrite the sentences. See if you can make your revisions even stronger than my suggestions. Many of the answers are neither right nor wrong, only stronger or weaker. With my Find and Refine Method, your computer points out opportunities for improvement, but only you can write in style.

3

PATCH UP PRONOUNS

Let's examine the lowly pronoun, the substitute for people, places, and things that have been previously specified. In the following sentence, the pronouns *he*, *her*, and *one* replace the names and things mentioned already: *John donned the hat he had bought after Shirley suffered frostbite on her ears for not wearing one.*

Pronouns don't seem worthy of an entire chapter in a book about creative writing, but trust me, every pronoun you use deserves your complete attention.

Pronouns may be similar to the dings and scrapes on your automobile. You see them so often that you don't see them anymore. If your car were for sale, though, potential buyers would inspect it from front to back bumper. Every pockmark, every little dent would stand out under the scrutiny of the potential purchaser. Pronouns are about the same. You know what you meant; pronoun become invisible to you, but to a skilled editor, unclear and incorrect pronouns catch attention every time. Grab that can of Bondo, and let's attack all those pronoun pockmarks until your manuscript has a smooth surface with no flaws.

First the Obvious

You know the standard pronouns, such as *I, me, he, she, it, her, him, its, we, us, you, they, their, one, who, whose, this, these, them*, and *those*, and even possessive ones, such as *his*, *hers*, *mine*, *ours*, *yours*, and *theirs*. While you may not know what to call them, you also know the reflexive pronouns, such as *myself*, *yourself*, *himself*, *herself*, *itself*, *yourselves*, and *themselves*. Nothing new, you say. There must be more. Aha! What about *there*? Also a pronoun, *there* can refer to an unspecified person, place, or thing, as in *Ahoy, there!* The word *there* can also be an undefined or indefinite pronoun, especially when it introduces a sentence.

We'll discuss the pronouns we call undefined or indefinite first, because in writing in style, undefined and indefinite pronouns can throw a wrench in the works.

Undefined (or Indefinite) Pronouns

Most of us use undefined pronouns when we speak and write, without ever considering the consequences. Undefined pronouns do not modify (define) a stated noun. They appear as innocent-looking uses of *there* and *it*, often at the beginning of a sentence or clause, and frequently followed by some form of the verb *to be*. Here are some examples of undefined pronouns:

1. *It* rained cats and dogs.
2. *There* was no reason to stay.
3. *It* was two o'clock.
4. When we arrived, *there* were four policemen at the scene of the crime.
5. *There* were three flaws in the contract.
6. Although I wanted to leave, *it* wasn't time yet.

Are undefined pronouns incorrect? No, not at all. As you can see, all the examples show no flaws in construction or grammar, but read on to see how you write in style when you reduce the volume of undefined pronouns.

#*^%$ Deleted

Undefined pronouns also call for passive voice (no action takes place), and wise contemporary authors avoid passive voice whenever possible. Undefined pronouns and passive voice have a place in literature, especially in the classics. "It was the best of times; it was the worst of times," wrote Dickens, who got paid by the word and had a reason to be verbose.

At times authors have valid reasons to delay revealing who did what. Sometimes writers choose to use an undefined pronoun and passive voice to change the rhythm of a sentence or paragraph. Again, I am not saying undefined pronouns never have a place. I am warning writers to be conscious of them, not to overuse them, and use them only when they are unavoidable.

Perhaps you'll understand some of the problem with undefined pronouns once I explain they are also expletives. Expletives? Exactly. Expletives are not always swearwords. Expletives are any words with no meaning. They are fillers. Like *damn* and *hell* and scatological references such as *shit*, expletives add words yet contribute nothing to the meaning or value of the sentence. Expletives are expendable, and when you write creatively, you'll toss away every unnecessary word as if it were a dirty paper towel.

When you delete undefined pronouns, you may find some of your sentences grow in length, but don't worry. Your verbs get stronger, so your writing will, too. Clean house occasionally. Always look for ways to make your writing sparkle with more scintillating descriptions and active verbs.

Let's reexamine the examples above and consider alternatives.

1. Original: It rained cats and dogs. Revision: Sheets of rain poured from the sky.
2. Original: There was no reason to stay. Revision: John watched Mary walk toward Jim and knew how the story would unfold. With a shake of his head, John grabbed his coat and left the party.
3. Original: It was two o'clock. Revision: Sam checked his watch and looked down the track for the two o'clock train.
4. Original: When we arrived, there were four policemen at the scene of the crime. Revision: When we arrived, four policemen shuffled around at the scene of the crime.
5. Original: There were three flaws in the contract. Revision: My attorney found three flaws in the contract.
6. Original: Although I wanted to leave, it wasn't time, yet. Revision: Although I wanted to leave, I knew I had to stay until after my wife left the apartment.

Notice that more powerful verbs emerge in the revisions. For more information on selecting strong verbs, see chapter five.

Tone it Down and Tune It Up

Too many instances of *there was*, *there were*, and *it was* result in repetition and static, lifeless verbs. Strong writers also show, rather than tell, but undefined pronouns tell; they do not show. When too many undefined pronouns appear in a manuscript, the writing becomes boring.

Although you do not have to delete every undefined pronoun, be conscious of them and judicious in their use. Consider each one an opportunity to write in style. When you catch undefined pronouns, replace them with concrete nouns and active verbs.

Undefined pronoun: There were four ways Jerry could knot his tie.

Better (eliminates needless words): Jerry could knot his tie four ways.

Undefined pronoun: It all began when someone knocked at the door.

Better (total recasting of sentence to make it more active and interesting): When someone knocked on Jerry's door in the middle of the night, he leaped out of the bed in a cold sweat.

It Was a Dark and Stormy Manuscript

Let's examine that last example, *It all began when someone knocked at the door.* Similar sentences appear in the opening lines of amateur work. Cease and desist! You have heard the classic opening line that begins with "It was a dark and stormy night." Do you know what the entire first sentence said? Here goes:

It was a dark and stormy night; the rain fell in torrents—except at occasional intervals, when it was checked by a violent gust of wind which swept up the streets (for it is in London that our scene lies), rattling along the housetops, and fiercely agitating the scanty

flame of the lamps that struggled against the darkness.
— Edward George Bulwer-Lytton, *Paul Clifford* (1830)

Before you assert that Bulwer-Lytton's writing must be good because some publisher bought his book, hear me out. The English Department of San Jose State University sponsors an annual Bulwer-Lytton contest that welcomes entries for the worst possible opening sentences. The university collected so many horrid, yet hilarious, assaults on the English language that Penguin Books has published at least five collections of them. Do you want a potential agent or publisher to laugh out loud at your opening line? You don't, if you are writing serious literature, so read on.

Find and Refine Method

When you are ready to write in style, you will use the Find function on your computer. Computer programs differ, but all will have a Find function. In most programs Control+F opens the Find window. Once you have the Find window, type in the word *there*. Examine each use of *there* and revise as many as possible that are undefined. When you finish, congratulate yourself.

Take a breath and then use the Find function to locate each usage of *it* and revise all that are undefined. Not all uses of either word will be undefined, so scrutinize each one. Use your skull, and you'll improve your skills.

To locate the most offensive undefined pronouns, the ones at the beginning of sentences, use the Replace function. Typing Control+H brings up the Replace window in my current Word program, but you may have to click on the Help button— usually a question mark at the top of the screen—to learn how to access this function in later versions of Word. The Replace window has an option at the bottom that says More. Click on it and check Match Case. Next type in *There* with a capital letter, and your computer will stop on every sentence that begins with *There*. Do the same for *It* with a capital. Study each sentence that begins with *There* or *It,* and you may be amazed at the number of sentences that begin with undefined pronouns. Consider each undefined pronoun to decide if you can replace the sentence with stronger writing.

Some of these pronouns may refer to a noun in the prior sentence, so not all will be undefined, as in this example: *On the table, a book lay open. It had a leather cover.* Learn to spot the difference between an undefined pronoun and a defined one.

Defined Pronouns

Let's talk about other pronouns, now.

Misused pronouns confuse readers, so avoid them. Pronouns that readers quickly comprehend refer to a recently stated noun, as in this sentence: *John tied his tie; he bought it at a thrift shop.* Here the pronoun *his* clearly refers to *John,* the previously stated proper noun, and *it* clearly refers to *tie,* the previously stated noun. Everything is clear to the reader.

Some people like to toss in a sentence that shows the pronoun before the noun, but this structure often confuses readers, and creative writers should do nothing to spoil the reader's enjoyment of a story. Here's an example of what some writers consider creative, but readers may have to stop reading, to figure out the meaning. *Although she was a pretty girl, Melissa never wore makeup.* When the sentence stands alone, readers may wait to reach the proper noun, *Melissa,* but when the sentence appears amid other sentences, readers get misled and have to back up to understand. Consider the following example: *The cardboard box stood in the corner beside Joanna. As she rubbed her feet near the fireplace, Elizabeth sighed into the cold air.*

While you read that example, you probably assumed on first read that *she* referred to Joanna, because Joanna was the person last mentioned before the pronoun. By the time you finish the sentence, though, you learn you were supposed to be thinking of Elizabeth. Wording that makes readers backtrack for comprehension also makes them aware that they are reading. Never jolt readers out of a story. Never make them have to look around at other sentences to understand the meaning of what they just read. Be consistent and clear in your pronoun use, and you keep readers informed, entertained, and immersed in the story.

Clear Pronouns

Okay, so when used best, pronouns modify the last stated noun. Examine the following sentence: *I found a dog on the street. It was cold and wet.* This sentence means the street was cold and wet, not the dog, because *street* was the last stated noun. If the author meant the dog was cold, the sentence should read this way: *I found a cold, wet dog on the street.* Or this way: *On the street, I found a dog. It was cold and wet.* You can find many ways to write the same thing, but be cautious with pronouns. Be certain that by placement in the sentence, the pronoun modifies the word you intended.

Along the same lines, personal pronouns modify the last stated name. Example: *Jim and Jake went to the supermarket. He wanted to buy beans.* The sentence means Jake wanted to buy beans, because Jake was the last name before the pronoun. Using two names and one pronoun muddies a sentence. Consider this clearer and stronger revision: *Jim and Jake went to the supermarket because Jake wanted to buy beans.*

Here's another example: *Mary sat beside Jane. She reached for her hand.* Who reached for whose hand? To keep readers clear, you may rewrite this way: *Mary sat beside Jane, who reached for Mary's hand.*

Remember, too, that pronouns must agree with the nouns they modify.

Wrong: Each person received their diplomas.
Right: Each person received a diploma *or* All the people received their diplomas.

Wrong: SouthBank offers free safe deposit boxes to their senior account holders.
Right: SouthBank offers free safe deposit boxes to its senior account holders.

Wrong: Every doctor (singular) must earn their (plural) degree.
Correct: Every doctor (singular) must earn his or her (singular) degree *or* All (plural) doctors must earn their (plural) degrees.

Did you notice the little trick that resolves the agreement issue? If you make your nouns plural, your pronouns are often gender neutral. Instead of writing *Every good person keeps his or her voter's registration current*, you can be politically correct and write in style by writing it this way: *All good people keep their voter's registration current.*

You Want to What?

You, a perfectly acceptable pronoun, gets us in trouble if we don't watch out. Used correctly it means someone other than ourselves, as in *You'd better take out this trash, or you won't get your allowance.* Some writers, though, perhaps out of fear of being too personal, use *you* (second person) when they mean *I* (first person). We do it all the time when we speak, so it weasels its way into our literature. Look for examples such as this: *When you first go to school, you feel afraid.* Would the sentence be stronger if the author admitted his or her own fear? *When I first went to school, I felt afraid.* You bet that's better!

Put the emphasis where it belongs, and readers will empathize. Be vague, and they will ignore your message. We don't want readers to disregard us, do we? Run a Find function throughout your manuscript and see if it has instances of *you* that would be better if rewritten into the personal *I*.

It Makes One Want to Cry

One, another vague pronoun, also adds unnecessary formality, at times, and it offers us yet an opportunity to write better. Avoid using the impersonal *one* for first person (I) or second person (you). Here are some examples of *one* used in weak or stilted ways.

Weak/stilted: One had to cover one's nose to avoid the smell.
Stronger: I had to cover my nose to avoid the smell.

Weak/stilted: If one paid attention, one could hear the small whine.
Stronger: If I paid attention, I could hear the small whine.

Weak/stilted: One easily discerns the solution to the mystery.
Stronger: Readers easily discern the solution to the mystery.

While We Are On This Subject

Consider the use of *this* and *these* in past-tense narrative. Used incorrectly, they jerk readers back and forth between past and present tense, which reminds them they are reading. Why? We use *this* or *these* when we are pointing out something in the present. Example: *These columns across the front of this building were manufactured in Greec*e. In dialogue, the sentence is fine, because we visualize something like a guide pointing out architecture to tourists, but strong writers avoid such usage in narrative. Read on to learn why.

In narrative the same sentence would not work as well, because when we speak or write of something we can no longer see, instead of *this* and *these*, we use *that, those,* or other pronouns that show distance between here and now and then and there. If writing narrative, a better way to write the example would be this: *The columns across the front of the building were manufactured in Greece.*

Good writers keep readers suspended in the world of literature. *This* and *these* used incorrectly bounce us out of the story.

In narrative choose pronouns or articles such as *that, those,* or *the* or otherwise revise the sentence.

Example: The boss was interested in this girl who had all the charm of a serpent.
Better: The boss was interested in the girl who had all the charm of a serpent.

Best (active voice): The boss took an active interest in the girl who had all the charm of a serpent.

Example: All the firefighters left their pants on the floor by their beds. This way, the men could jump into their pants if the alarm sounded.
Better: All the firefighters left their pants on the floor by their beds, so the men could jump into their pants if the alarm sounded.
Or: All the firefighters left their pants on the floor by their beds. That way, the men could jump into their pants if the alarm sounded.

Myself and Other Reflexive Pronouns

Here's one more little detail to remember, a little step into what's right and wrong. Reflexive pronouns such as *himself*, *herself*, or *myself* cannot replace a first-person pronoun.

Incorrect: Write to the chairman or myself.
Correct: Write to the chairman or me.

I see the *myself* error frequently, perhaps because writers assume it sounds astute to use reflexive pronouns rather than saying words such as *me* and *I*.

The use of *myself* is correct when you do something to yourself, as in this example: *I hurt myself.* The issue is a grammar issue, not necessarily a creative style issue, but what the heck, let's get everything right. Tell your computer to find *myself* and other reflexive pronouns wherever they appear in your manuscript and make reflexive pronouns appear only when used correctly.

This or That Concept

Allow me to address another grammar issue, one that even the most educated writers do not always catch and repair in their work. Pronouns such as *that* or *this* cannot refer to a concept. Pronouns must modify nouns, not ideas. Here is an example of a pronoun used incorrectly to refer to a concept: *Steve ate oatmeal every morning. That is how he lowered his cholesterol.* A correct version may go like this: *Steve ate oatmeal every morning, a method by which he lowered his cholesterol.* Or: *Steve ate oatmeal every morning. That one change in his diet lowered his cholesterol.*

Dialogue is a Different Animal

Most of the information I give you in this book applies to narrative, rather than dialogue, because people speak in ways that reveal their character, and they do not always speak in perfect English. Executives, prim people, or someone trying to act above his or her station in life might use a reflexive pronoun such as *myself* incorrectly, in an attempt to sound highfalutin. Foppish men might use a reflexive pronoun in a haughty way, to avoid saying *you*. Dialogue is slippery, and we must use ploys to reveal character through dialogue. When your computer stops on a pronoun that one of your characters has used in dialogue, think twice before changing it. When you write dialogue, be sure to use pronouns the way the character would, but in narrative, use pronouns correctly.

Allow me to digress for a moment, because I used the word *highfalutin*, a word I often see misspelled in manuscripts. *Highfalutin* means pretentious, grandiose, or pompous. It is not two words, and it does not require an apostrophe at the end. If you use *highfalutin* in a manuscript, be sure to use it and spell it correctly, or you will look lowfalutin, as if there were such a word.

Ready to Write in Style?

Okay, folks, I've given you the tools you need. You know how to spot pronouns when you see them, and you have the computer to help you find undefined and reflexive pronouns, so you can choose whether to rewrite the sentences in which they appear. Below are some exercises to ensure you understand the basics of using pronouns to your best advantage. After the exercises, I give potential rewrites. Yours don't have to match mine; yours may be even better. Type the sentences below into your computer and use the Find and Refine Method to uncover opportunities to write in style.

1. It was the kind of day that made you want to kick back and climb into a hammock.
2. All around me, there were these shards of glass.
3. Under the circumstances, there was only one thing one could do to improve the situation.
4. When you first enter the building, there is an ornate foyer where one hangs his coat.
5. My allergies acted up. That was why I had to leave.
6. The donations were sent to my wife and myself.
7. Before my father passed away, he was crazy about this dog named Lucky.
8. There have to be at least three ways to answer the question.
9. This man who controlled the budget voted against the plan.

10. The first time you hear your parents argue, you think they are going to get a divorce.

Possible rewrites:

1. Because of the chirping birds and warm breezes, the day made me want to kick back and climb into a hammock.
2. All around me, I saw shards of glass.
3. Under the circumstances, only one thing would improve the situation.
4. When visitors first enter the building, they can hang their coats in the ornate foyer.
5. My allergies acted up, so I had to leave.
6. People sent the donations to my wife and me.
7. Before my father passed away, he was crazy about his dog named Lucky.
8. The question must have at least three answers.
9. The man who controlled the budget voted against the plan.
10. The first time I heard my parents argue, I thought they are going to get a divorce.

Your Manu-slip Is Showing

Okay, enough of the hard work. Earlier I promised to give you a few typos, flaws, or other mistakes I've spotted in unedited manuscripts. I have copied them as I saw them, warts and all, although I changed or deleted character names. Some of the excerpts below defy description or become so lengthy you will wallow in the mire, but no matter what, you will learn something from reading them, so here we go:

- This novel is guaranteed to suffice the most intriguing minds in which our society have in relevant to the "Playerlistic Exuberance" of today's insubordinated urban youths and young adults alike. [This sentence is guaranteed to turn away anyone who reads it.]
- Excerpt from a letter sent to my editing firm: I am interested in working with your firm as a freelancer. I am currently an English teacher and have read a lot of compostitions (sic), research papers, and essays of young high school students. . . . I also have written articles for the local newspaper when it comes to school events. . . . I also feel like I have the experience in proofreading and editing since I do this everyday (sic) in my job. [Need I say the person who wrote the letter did not get the job?]
- The intoxication of love, of lust what could any consequences be to this? He knew too well. [What could the sentence mean? I know not well.]
- But at that brief moment in time, a nanosecond appeared to stretch into infinity, and he fervently prayed to that unknown protector of fools and little children, that he be blown aside by the on-rushing train, which appeared like a nightmarish vision - it's shining headlight heralding a Cyclop from Hades. [With about fifty words in the third sentence in the prologue, complete with errors throughout, apparently the author forgot to write tight.]
- It was the best sort of summer night, when you're not sure whether you're warm or you're cool, and it's all stars and wisps of sounds of people walking out, far enough away you don't have to worry about seeing

them but close enough you can hear them now and then, and if you want you can start wondering about who they are and what their lives are like, which is always a pleasure. [After trying to decipher a seventy-four-word sentence, readers can start wondering about whether to keep reading.]

- They were still groggy from the drug that puts muscles to sleep and keeps you wide-awake trying to move them.

4

FLUSH YOUR SYSTEM OF ADVERBS

We learned in school that adverbs, which often appear as words with "ly" at the end—such as *suddenly, ruefully, excitedly, swiftly, slowly, quickly, immediately,* and others—are good words that give strength to verbs, adjectives, and other adverbs. Our lessons encouraged us to use all the parts of speech correctly, and if we did, we got good grades. We learned to sprinkle a little of everything into our essays and book reports. I agree; we should.

Adverbs, though, like additives for your gas tank, help a little, but if you add too high a percentage, your engine (and your writing) conks out. Let's talk about ways to keep your writing from stalling.

I do not mean to say you can never use an adverb, but remember my promise: adverbs almost always indicate an opportunity to improve your writing.

Uh-oh, *almost* and *always* are adverbs.

How can you possibly write without adverbs? You could rewrite most sentences and delete the adverbs. In the previous sentence I might have said, "How can you write without adverbs?" The revised sentence, without the use of *possibly,* is stronger. Are you catching on now? What? *Now* is another sneaky adverb, so I could have said, "Are you catching on?"

I would have saved my ink and your time. It never ends, does it?

I'll talk about the sneaky adverbs later. First I'll concentrate on obvious ones, the ones that end in "ly." Of the obvious adverbs, *suddenly* stands out as most overused in the manuscripts I edit. Editors joke among themselves that a novelist is allowed one *suddenly* per book. Inexperienced writers may think the word *suddenly* adds excitement, but it slows the pace and takes away from the thrill of the story.

For example, you've put three characters in the woods. They're lost; the sun is setting; they have one small bottle of water among them and no food. They want to find a way out before the light disappears and a cold night chills them. You've set the scene through action and dialogue, and you have us readers on the edges of our seats. Everyone hopes Joe, John, and Marie spot their original path and find their way home. Good writers, however, turn up the tension whenever they can, right? You decide to make John fall and sprain his ankle, which adds tension, because it slows the group even more. How will you write that scene? An inexperienced writer might try this way: *Suddenly, John fell and twisted his ankle.*

While nothing in that sentence cries for grammar repair, we're discussing creative writing. What would make the scene stronger? Consider this rewrite:

John pointed. "I think I see light over there." He bolted toward a distant break in the trees.

Marie threw out a hand. "No! Wait! That's not—"

John's foot snagged a root, and he sprawled to the ground. "Rats!" He grabbed his ankle in pain. "I think I broke it."

Marie leaned over him. "I tried to tell you, it's just a little clearing. It's not the way out. Can you walk?"

John held Marie's arm for support and stood. "There." He took a deep breath. With his next step, though, he crumpled back to the ground.

In my version of the scene, I offer seven chances to use *suddenly*: when John points, when he sees the light, when he runs toward the break, when Marie throws out a hand, when his foot snags a root, when he falls to the ground, and when he falls the second time. How many times did I use the word? None. Did you miss it? Not at all. Readers understand which things happened suddenly.

Consider Your Motivation

Mary quickly took off her shoes. Perhaps better: *Mary took off her shoes*. Wait. Something's missing. Let's talk about the reason you wanted to use the adverb in the first place, and you'll see that changing the verb might be the answer, rather than simply deleting the adverb. For example, you might have rewritten the sample sentence this way: *Mary ripped off her shoes*. With the verb change, we know Mary took her shoes off quickly, without the use of an adverb.

Although many sentences grow stronger with the deletion of an adverb, don't zap adverbs without first pondering why you used it. Perhaps you thought the verb wasn't strong enough without the modifying adverb.

For example, you might write *He walked slowly toward the front door*. Before you deep-six the adverb, ponder why you sensed that *walked* wasn't strong enough by itself. If you wanted to indicate that a character was not enthusiastic about leaving, what strong verb might make your point? Lack of enthusiasm isn't enough. What motivated the character? What would his walk indicate to readers? If you want to imply nonchalance, you could use *He strolled toward the front door.* If you wanted to indicate arrogance, consider *He sauntered toward the front door.* If he did not want to leave, try *He stumbled toward the front door, looking back with every step.*

Every time you catch an adverb while you edit, stop and think. Adverbs indicate a possible chance to choose more powerful, visual verbs that help you write in style, so your writing grows in strength.

Although Stephen King wrote, "Adverbs are not your friends," I suggest that adverbs *can* be your friends. Use them to locate sentences with weak verbs. Make your verbs stronger, and when you do, you can delete the adverbs.

I've Said Repeatedly . . .

The same rule applies to adverbs attached to dialogue as part of an attribution (a tag that attributes the dialogue to a character). For example, look at this snippet: *"I'm not sure I passed the test," Virgil said nervously.* In this case, *Virgil said nervously* is the tag, the attribution. Readers don't get a visual image from an attribution that tells, rather than shows. When you replace the adverb with action that shows what the reader is doing, you improve the scene. *Virgil's hands shook when he tried to open the paper to read his grade. "I'm not sure I passed the test," he said.* Show readers what Virgil does, and they surmise that he is nervous.

Even though I tell you to write tight, it doesn't mean always write short. When you describe the action—show readers, instead of telling them—even if you use a few more words, you add power to the story.

Hopefully You'll Remember This Rule

Some speakers and writers misuse *hopefully*, but I am hopeful you will not. The problem stems from the fact that by its misuse, many people believe *hopefully* means *it is hoped*, as in *Hopefully she will win the tournament.* In actuality, *hopefully* means *in a hopeful manner.* To be correct, it must apply to a person, as in this example: *After years of practice, she approached the tournament hopefully.* Promise me, please, that you will not write sentences such as this one: *Hopefully I'll find a publisher.*

A good editor won't let a misuse of *hopefully* pass, not even once, much less several times within the same manuscript, and if I see it used incorrectly once in a manuscript, I can lay bets it will appear again and again.

When tempted to use *hopefully*, read the sentence aloud. Rephrase it. Are you saying the character is hopeful, or are you saying I, she, or he hopes? If you mean the latter, rewrite the sentence and delete *hopefully*.

Are You Repetitiously Redundant?

We know adverbs frequently signal an opportunity to rewrite and write in style, but sometimes they are redundant. Redundant adverbs permeate clichés, for example, which should come as no surprise. For example, look at these sentences: *She gently caressed her baby's head. He suddenly jumped off the bridge. The wind whistled noisily through the tunnel.* In all those examples, the adverbs are redundant, because you can't caress something without being gentle. You can't jump slowly. You can't have a quiet whistle. Even so, notice how many times you'll see *gently* associated with *caress* and *suddenly* linked with *jumped*. Do you get the picture?

Delete the redundant adverbs, and you write in style.

Don't Create New Adverbs

Some people create their own adverbs, as if the ones we already have aren't bad enough. I've edited out adverbs such as *obliteratingly*. Help! When you run a spell check on your document and find a word that is not in your computer dictionary, it may not be a word. Look it up in *Merriam-Webster*, and if the word still doesn't appear, ditch it. Although creative writing allows us to coin a word on occasion, use the technique to create a good new verb or noun only, please.

Author Intrusion

Adverbs can also imply author intrusion, sometimes called editorializing, which is a no-no. Author intrusion occurs when anything implies the personal feelings of the author, rather than showing an unbiased description.

> **Example:** Luckily (or fortunately), the car was unlocked.
> **Better:** He found the car unlocked and exhaled in relief.

The wording in the first example implies that the author found the situation fortunate. In the second, better rewrite, we see that the character found the situation fortunate. See the difference?

Study any use of *hopefully, thankfully* or *fortunately*. In narrative, they could indicate author intrusion, and if so, you must eliminate them.

As long as we're talking about author intrusion, although *of course* is not an adverb, I sometimes see the two-word intrusion, as in the following example: *Of course, the door was locked.* Can you see that the author is implying he or she knew such bad luck would befall the character? Delete *of course* wherever it appears in narrative, unless you are writing in first person.

Avoid Qualifiers

We talked about obvious adverbs, the ones that end in "ly." Now let's examine subtle adverbs, the ones that sneak into our narrative and stall our efforts.

Adverbs such as *rather, very, pretty* (to mean *very*), *somewhat,* and *somehow* wiggle their way into our language every day. If you think of them as grimy little worms, though, you would not want to add them to your gas tank, right?

Qualifiers such as those listed above drain power from your prose. I also call them dampeners, and they act the way governors act on vehicle accelerators. Does anyone remember governors? I don't know if anyone uses them anymore, but fleet owners used to put the devices on vehicles so drivers could not go over the speed limit, even if they tried. Trucks lasted longer, and companies saved on gasoline, reduced the number of wrecks, and avoided having speeding tickets attributed to their vehicles. Governors work fine for slowing down trucks, but do you want to slow down your prose? No, you want to strengthen it.

Instead of saying something is pretty hot, say it is ardent, fiery, torrid, sultry, blistering, boiling, broiling, burning, heated, red-hot, scalding, scorching, sizzling, or sweltering. As you pick out qualifiers in your work, consider them an opportunity to choose one precise word, instead of two limp ones.

Ninety-nine percent of qualifiers such as *somewhat, rather, kind of, sort of, a bit,* and *somehow,* are superfluous, especially in narrative. Delete them, and you write in style.

Example: Somehow Anita managed to free her hands from the rope.
Better: Anita managed to free her hands from the rope.

Example: Bernice found the note to be rather annoying.

Better: Bernice found the note annoying.

I Hate This One Very Much

While we're on the subject of qualifiers, let me address my favorite adverb to hate: *very*.

One of my creative writing teachers once said, "Every time you see *very*, think of it as the word *damn*." Why *damn*? Like *damn*, *very* adds nothing but letters to the sentence, even though we think it adds emphasis.

We do better to choose one strong word, instead or two weaker ones. For example, instead of *very dry*, use *parched*. Instead of *very wet*, choose *drenched*.

Writers improve their work when they delete *very* whenever it appears. You can become even more creative, though, if you examine every use of *very* and consider it an opportunity to choose a more creative adjective instead of the one that *very* had modified.

Example: After fishing all day, Curt was very tired.

Better: After fishing all day, Curt was exhausted.

Even better: After fishing all day, Curt found that every muscle in his body ached.

Now and Then, an Odd One

Then, when used as an adverb, can often be deleted, like many other adverbs, without changing the meaning of a sentence. *We bought a car and then bought car insurance* can be written as *We bought a car and car insurance*. When I edit, I must take out more uses of *then* than almost any other word.

When you use the Find and Refine Method to find uses of *then*, I'll bet you'll delete a high volume of them as well.

While you search for which uses of *then* you want to delete, remember to avoid using *then* to begin a sentence.

Incorrect: I sat for my bar exam. Then I went into private practice.
Correct: I sat for my bar exam, and then I went into private practice.

Here's another important point about the adverb *then*; it is not a conjunction. If you use it as a conjunction, you've made a typical mistake I find in many manuscripts I edit.

Incorrect: Aidan apologized, then sent flowers.
Correct: Aidan apologized and then sent flowers.

More Adverbs That Sneak In

We discussed a few sly adverbs that can squeak by us. I have a few more adverbs up my sleeve that have an even more obtrusive effect on our narrative prose. The words are *now, ago, today, yesterday, tomorrow, tonight,* and other words used as adverbs in narrative. Let me give you an example: *Michael looked forward to going home tonight to his evening highball.* The sentence looks harmless to the uninitiated, but you already know about words that have a subtle push-pull between present and past tense, because we discussed it in the chapter on pronouns. Examine the words again: *now, ago, today, yesterday, tomorrow, tonight.* All these words imply present tense.

Examine this sentence of dialogue: *"I will see you tomorrow."* In dialogue the sentence works fine, because dialogue takes place in the present. Rewrite the sentence in narrative, though, and it might come out like this: *He said he would see her tomorrow.* Feel the little pull going on? The sentence is better if rewritten this way: *He said he would see her the next day.* Here are some other examples and preferable rewrites:

Disconcerting: The street was quieter now.
Better: The street grew quiet.

Disconcerting: They bought bagels two days ago.
Better: They had bought bagels two days before.

Disconcerting: The meeting time was four o'clock today.
Better: The meeting time was four o'clock that day.

Disconcerting: He spotted his ex-wife at the mall yesterday.
Better: The day before, he spotted his ex-wife at the mall.

Disconcerting: He needed sleep before his appointment tomorrow.
Better: He needed sleep before his appointment the next day.

Disconcerting: She slept longer than usual tonight.
Better: She slept longer than usual that night.

Disconcerting: John wrote his father a letter and mailed it a day ago, but now he's sorry.

Better: John wrote his father a letter and mailed it a day before, but now he's sorry.

Disconcerting: Larry had three things he had to do today.
Better: Larry had three things he had to do that day.

Disconcerting: Tomorrow Richard was going to pick up his son at the train station.
Better: Richard was going to pick up his son at the train station the next day.

Disconcerting: Nancy used to live here, but now she lives in Washington.
Better: Nancy used to live here, but she moved to Washington.

When you're ready to write in style, access the Find function on your computer. Type in "ly" with a space after it for the first search to find the obvious adverbs. Perform another search using "ly" followed by a comma ("ly,"). Study each "ly" word to see if it is an adverb, if it is necessary, and if it signals an opportunity to write in style. Each time your computer identifies an adverb, scrutinize it. Ask yourself the following questions:

- Is the adverb redundant?
- Is it correct?
- Is it necessary?
- Is it a real word?
- Would the sentence be stronger if I delete the adverb?
- Did I use this adverb because my verb is weak?

- What happens if I change my verb?
- Did I use this adverb because I speak this way, but in narrative the adverb is unnecessary?

Think about each potential change. You may decide to leave in an occasional adverb, but each one you delete, each sentence you rewrite, helps you write in style.

After you have deleted as many obvious adverbs as possible, attack the tricky ones. One at a time, type in each of the less-obvious adverbs. Go down the list below, each time running a Find through the manuscript. Whenever you find one of these words used as an adverb, especially in narrative, delete it, and you'll improve your style.

- Ago
- Almost
- Always
- Now
- Pretty (when it means very)
- Rather
- Somehow
- Somewhat
- Today
- Then
- Very
- Yesterday

Ready to Write in Style?

Below are some exercises to ensure you understand adverbs. Type the exercises into your computer and use the Find and Refine Method—that is, use the Find function—to find all the "ly" adverbs and then the other adverbs in the list that don't end in "ly." Decide which ones are worthy of staying and which ones signal an opportunity for improvement. After the exercises, I give potential rewrites. Yours don't have to match mine; yours may be even better than mine.

1. Marty gently held the baby to his chest.
2. Today is the day Ken had an appointment with the doctor to see if he was seriously ill.
3. Four years ago, Ruth gave birth to a newborn baby and was fairly ecstatic about the somewhat unique experience.
4. Eric had just now discovered the importance of having a genuinely strong positive attitude.
5. We have to buy an ironing board, and then we will be perfectly ready to move into our own apartment.
6. Although somewhat bedraggled, she somehow managed to look really good after she came in from the rain.
7. He gaily tipped his hat, then bowed deeply and smiled broadly.
8. Jane spoke wistfully about the pretty good time she had at the beach.
9. Harold almost always calls his mother and warmly tells her he loves her before he leaves town.
10. When the Scottish terrier barked excitedly at a complete stranger, Gerald scolded his dog rather strongly.

Possible rewrites:
1. Marty cradled the baby to his chest.
2. Ken, fearful his cough might indicate a serious illness, visited the doctor.

3. Four years earlier, Ruth had given birth. She still felt ecstatic about the experience.

4. Eric discovered the importance of maintaining a positive attitude.

5. We must buy an ironing board, after which we will be ready to move into our apartment.

6. Although bedraggled, she appeared composed after she came in from the rain.

7. He tipped his hat, bowed, and smiled.

8. Jane spoke wistfully about the good time she had at the beach. (See? I allow one adverb here and there.)

9. Harold always calls his mother and tells her he loves her before he leaves town.

10. When the Scottish terrier barked at a stranger, Gerald scolded his dog.

Whoops! Your Manu-slip Is Showing

Just for fun, here are some actual examples of overused, incorrect, misplaced, unclear, or unnecessary adverbs found in unedited manuscripts, with all the other errors left intact, as well.

- He fidgeted restlessly. [Could he fidget restfully next time, please?]
- He yawned, lackadaisically looking without expression.
- The camp was nestled comfortably in the woods.
- "Yeah, lots of luck," the assistant muttered pessimistically. [Adverbs in attributions such as this example often are unnecessary, redundant, or incorrect.]

- His tan skin was still covered with goose-bumps, when the ring of the phone, like a mosquito in the mist at sunset after a hot steamy August evening rain, flew in from the bedroom and annoyingly hovered over his head, disturbing his self-indulgence. [This sentence flew into my eyes and annoyed my reading.]

- In turn, each slipper had then been tied to the merchant's feet via a tangled web of fishing line, and with each and every step, the Coat of Many Soles jumped out to wriggle menacingly like a school of rubber guard eels; hopefully instilling a measure of awe and respect into his intended victims. [The coat was hopeful? How smart of the coat!]

- The squalling winds whistled alertingly, letting its relentless pressure be known. [Alert writers avoid coined adverbs even more relentlessly than they avoid actual adverbs.]

5

REPLACE WORN-OUT VERBS

Verbs act like engines in sentences. Powerful verbs move your stories forward, but worn-out verbs, like old engines, spit, sputter, and die. In the process of powering up your pronouns and adverbs in the previous chapters, you may have added verve to some verbs. Now we'll concentrate on the remaining verbs in your manuscript and energize them, too.

In this chapter we'll discuss action verbs versus linking verbs and active voice as opposed to passive voice. We'll talk about participles and gerunds, too, but don't let those terms scare you. As you'll soon learn, I have an easy way for you to find and replace them, regardless of whether you know what to call them. Relax and enjoy the ride.

The Weakest Link

Linking verbs: What on earth are they, and what's wrong about them? I'm glad you asked. Linking verbs state that something is or is not the same as something else. While nothing is wrong with them grammatically, for the purposes of creative writing, they are weak verbs because they don't show any action.

Linking verbs include all forms of *to be*, plus other verbs, including the following:

- Appear
- Become
- Feel
- Grow
- Look
- Remain
- Smell
- Seem
- Stand
- Sound
- Taste
- Turn

Linking verbs such as those in the list contain no motion; therefore they add words and weaken writing.

Examples
The book was dusty.
The driver felt sleepy.
Basketball players appear to be eight feet tall.
Ezekiel did not seem to care about me.
Bill stood in the doorway.
Chicken soup tastes like heaven.
Green maple leaves turn into red ones in the fall.

To improve your writing, convert as many linking verbs as possible into action verbs or other strong forms that show, rather than tell. Help readers "see" or "experience" the information.

Examples

I blew dust from the book.

The driver's eyelids kept closing, his head nodding toward his chest.

Basketball players often duck to avoid hitting the top of a door frame.

Ezekiel looked away when I walked over.

Maple leaves shed their green color with fall and glow bright red instead.

To Be or Not to Be

To be a good writer or not to be? That is the question. When you see the verb *to be* in any of its forms (*be, was, were, are, is, am*), change the verb to an active form, and you'll improve your style. Instead of *She was walking her dog,* consider *She walked her dog.* No, you cannot eliminate every use of *to be,* but each sentence you write in style helps the total manuscript.

Many writers rely on the verb *to be* to carry too many sentences. When writers make that mistake, their words become repetitive and the pace slows.

> **Example:** Her complexion was pale, and she was wearing heavy makeup to cover it.
> **Better:** She wore heavy makeup to hide her pale complexion.

Be open to change! Strive for improvement! Write in style! Use action verbs, rather than linking verbs. When you replace weak verbs that show, rather than tell, your sentences and descriptions may grow in length, but your writing grows in strength. Here are more examples of sentences that rely on linking verbs that tell, rather than show:

Harry appeared to have an interest in Jaye, but she knew he was married. He was always flirting with her and flattering her. In return, she was always trying to seem disinterested, but she was beginning to have feelings for him, as well.

A complete recast that relies on dialogue and action verbs to show, rather than tell that Harry had an interest in Jaye:

Harry laughed louder than required and brushed Jaye's shoulder with his fingers. "You're the funniest person I ever knew," he said. "I find you alluring."

Jaye nodded. "It's always nice to see you here."

"Jaye?" Harry sidled up even closer and lowered his voice. "Would you like to get a drink after the meeting?"

"Thanks, but I'm sure your wife expects you at home." Jaye turned away, but glanced back at Harry's departing figure and sighed.

Passive Voice Stalls at the Starting Line

Before I speak about passive voice, let me make sure everyone understands the difference between tense and voice.

Tense refers to whether something takes place in the past, present, or future. The following sentence is in future tense. *I will write better.* The following sentence is in present tense: *I write better.* The following sentence is in past tense: *I wrote better.*

Voice, however, in its simplest explanation, refers the order of the words in a sentence. It's not an issue of correct or incorrect grammar; it's a syntactical issue.

You can have sentences in past, present, or future tense that are in either passive or active voice. Strive to use active voice whenever possible, though, no matter what tense you use. Confused? Don't be. Read on to see some examples.

Past tense expresses something that happened in the past, as in this sentence: *Ritchie hung his socks out to dry.* That sentence is in past tense and active voice. *Ritchie* is the subject that performed the action. *Hung* is the verb, the action. The object, *socks*, shows us what *Ritchie* hung out. I have no qualms with past, present, or future tense in active voice. Passive voice in any tense, however, is another story.

Passive voice sometimes appears in convoluted sentences, as in these examples:

- The socks were hung out to dry.
- The socks were hung out to dry by Ritchie.

Notice how the object—*socks*—and the action, the verb—*were hung*—both come before the person who did the action (the subject—*Ritchie*). Often, but not always, the word *by* tips writers to the fact that the sentence is passive, rather than active. In the first example of passive voice, *The socks were hung out to dry*, we never find out who performed the action, who hung the socks out to dry. Like other weak verbal styles, passive voice can lean on linking verbs, a dead giveaway that you have an opportunity to improve your writing and write in style.

Passive voice has its purpose, when used in moderation. In a murder mystery, for example, if you don't want readers to know who did something, you may find yourself tempted to use a passive-voice sentence here and there, as in this example: *The corpse was dropped near the back do*or. You may think if you wrote the sentence in active voice, you would have to put in the killer's name. Aha! Not so, my dear Watson!

You can still make it active without giving away any secrets, as in this rewrite: *The killer dropped the corpse near the back door.* What if the investigators don't know if a crime has occurred at all? In that case, *The corpse lay near the back door* helps the writer remain neutral about who caused the death while making the sentence active, rather than passive.

Why is active voice better?

Active voice is direct writing, whereas passive voice adds words, slows the pace, and often creates complicated sentences. Examine the difference between these two sentences:

Passive: The kite was given to the boy.
Active: Santa gave the boy a kite.

Most successful contemporary writers shun passive voice and use active voice almost exclusively. Active voice makes the writing clearer, adds action, and often eliminates extra words.

Here's an interesting fact: Dickens and other writers of classics had an incentive to use wordy phrases and passive voice. Publishers of that era paid writers by the word. Longer books brought bigger payments to the authors.

Today people have less time to read, and our attention spans are shorter. In addition, long books cost more to produce, so publishers demand tighter writing. I could say, "We don't get paid by the word; we get paid to write succinctly," but that would be passive voice. Instead, I'll say this: "Publishers don't pay us by the word; they pay us to write succinctly."

A Few Verbs to Avoid

I'll address some verbs that appear acceptable, but when replaced with stronger ones, the writing grows bolder. As a quick rundown, whenever you find yourself using any form of the following verbs, you may have an opportunity to write in style and make it stronger:

- Was/are/were/am/is/been
- Do/Did
- Place
- Put
- Would
- Could
- Has/had
- Got
- Thought/felt/believed
- Realized
- Take/took

I will discuss each one in detail.

Cannot Be Emphasized Enough

Yes, I addressed why strong writers avoid all forms of *to be*, but I repeat it here for emphasis. All forms of *to be* (*be, is, was, were, are, being, been*, etc.) indicate telling, rather than showing, and all forms of *to be* are linking verbs, rather than action verbs. Ponder each use of the verb *to be* and find strong ways to rewrite without it, whenever possible.

Do You See What I See?

English offers a splendid choice of verbs with razzle-dazzle, sizzle, and power. Think of verbs such as these: Instead of the word *stop* as a verb, writers can choose *interrupt, discontinue, halt, pause, check,* or even *arrest.* In comparison to its alternates, the word *stop* is a yawner.

Many verbs lie down and feign death in inactive sentences with unclear meanings. The verb *do* is one of the worst offenders.

A potential client once e-mailed me, "Do you do articles?" I pondered the question and responded, "Do I do articles? The answer depends on what you mean. Do I write articles? Do I edit articles? Do I assign articles? Do I create article ideas? Please be specific in your question, and I will be glad to answer."

Notice that in my response, I used *do* often, but in a way that clarifies the message.

Be careful when you use *do.* It has far too many meanings. *Merriam-Webster,* the dictionary that the producers of *The Chicago Manual of Style* prefer, lists forty definitions of the word, along with many more uses of *do* in idioms. For that reason, be sure when you use it that its meaning is clear. Look how many ways you can interpret the same sentence, when vague words appear.

Vague: Please undo my shoelaces.
Clear: Please untie my shoelaces.
Please take the knot out of my shoelaces.
Please take the shoelaces out of my shoes.

Vague: Smith and Company did the project.
Clear: Smith and Company performed the construction for the project.

Smith and Company performed the engineering for the project.

Smith and Company installed the heating, ventilation, and air conditioning at the project.

Smith and Company oversaw the project.

Smith and Company designed the project.

Vague: Who did the set for the play?
Clear: Who designed the set for the play?
Who built the set for the play?

Vague: What will Mary do after graduation?
Clear: What profession will Mary enter after graduation?
Where will Mary live after graduation?

Did

Did is another form of *do*. Look at these two sentences and decide which one portrays more strength:

- Whenever Harry did the mambo, he thrilled the crowd.
- Whenever Harry danced the mambo, he thrilled the crowd.

Whenever you see *did* in your manuscript, stop and contemplate what stronger verb might replace it.

Places, Everyone

Place is another vague verb that doesn't give a good visual picture to readers. To make matters worse, it can also be a noun, and the use of *place* as a verb and a noun leads to repetition, which bores readers.

Replace *place* with stronger verbs that give a visual impression as well as show the subject's emotions or intention.

> **Vague:** Roz placed the hat on her head.
> **Visual and visceral**: Roz slammed the hat on her head.
> Roz jammed the hat on her head.
> Roz settled the hat on her head.
> Roz tugged the hat on her head.

> **Vague:** Jim placed his hand on Jan's shoulder.
> **Visual and visceral:** Jim slid his arm around Jan's shoulder.
> Jim gripped Jan's shoulder.
> Jim rested the weight of his arm on Jan's shoulder.

See the nuances of stronger verbs? In the rewrites that make the sentences visual and visceral, we get a sense of Roz's intentions and feelings in the first set of examples. In the second, we derive a sense of the meaning behind Jim's action.

Would You Mind?

The appearance of the auxiliary verb *would* also gives writers an opportunity to write in style. In the manuscripts I evaluate, I see *would* overused so often that I want to scream. Sometimes it is misused, and sometimes writers don't remember that one or two auxiliary verbs set the tense, and the rest can return to the simple past tense.

Would is the past tense of *will*. Use it the following ways:

1. After a statement of desire, request, or advice: *I wish you would play tennis with me.*
2. To make a polite request: *Would you take this bag?*
3. To indicate uncertainty: *The temperature would seem to be getting cooler.*

Avoid using *would* too often in other forms, such as this sentence: *On weekdays, I would take the bus to work.* Use the past tense of the main verb instead. *On weekdays, I took the bus to work.*

Caution: *I'd, she'd,* and *he'd* hide the use of *I would, she would,* and *he would* and imitate contractions used for *I had, she had,* and *he had,* so they can lead to repetition.

Some writers use *would* correctly the first time, but forget to turn down the heat and switch to past tense. Here's an example:

Repetitious: We would like you to take the seminar on accounting, and then we would like to see you join the firm as a junior accountant. You would make a good entry-level salary.

Better: We would like you to take the seminar on accounting and join our firm as a junior accountant. You will make a good entry-level salary.

Any repetition avoided equals more stylish writing.

I Had One More Suggestion

Another weak verb that writers overuse is *had.* In past perfect (completed action), use *had* once or twice and then switch to past tense. Example: *Michael had always liked bananas.*

He ate them regularly. The first sentence is past perfect; the second is past, but readers understand that the action is not taking place anymore.

The Perfect Past

You may have heard a teacher refer to past-perfect tense as the pluperfect tense, but don't worry about what to call it. All you have to remember is that past perfect applies to sentences that show that the entire action was completed in the past. Example: *Johnny had gone to a neighborhood school.* The use of past perfect (*had gone*) implies that Johnny no longer goes to the neighborhood school. The action was completed in the past.

In fiction, most flashbacks show up in past perfect tense. Example: *Ezra thought back to his teen years, when he had been the brunt of every joke in his school.*

Past perfect tense is formed with the past participle of a verb and the auxiliary *had*, as *had learned* in this sentence: *He had learned to type by the time the semester was over.*

Even though the use of past perfect (*had* plus another verb) breaks no rules of grammar, be cautious and aware when you use it, because it can represent a missed opportunity to write in style. A few mentions of *had* go a long way and become repetitious, especially in contractions, such as *she'd* and *he'd*.

If a passage requires past perfect, one or two mentions of *had* set up the passage as past perfect, and the next verbs can be past tense.

Repetitious: John had called his girlfriend that morning. He had said they'd see each other that night.
Better: John had called his girlfriend that morning. He said they would see each other that night.

On-Stage or Off?

I object to the use of past perfect tense in creative writing because past perfect refers to things that have already happened, as if offstage, and narrative (telling) must explain it. In narrative, the writer tells, rather than shows that portion of the story. Authors should always try to show, rather than tell. Keep the action on-stage, where readers watch the story unfold. Instead of writing something like the following example, consider the possible rewrite that follows.

Weak: Greta got out of her car at Travelers Square. She had been to the square before, when she had been a little girl. She had walked the wide cement sidewalk that bordered the area and had wished she had enough money to shop in the craft stalls tucked under the oak trees.

Stronger: Greta stepped out of her car at Travelers Square and remembered an earlier visit, when she was young. Her mind raced back to the time her patent leather shoes strolled the wide cement sidewalk that bordered the area. She recalled her longing to have cash in her little pockets to buy crafts at the stalls tucked under the oak trees.

If *had* creeps into writing too often, consider ways to change to past tense, rather than past perfect. Rewrite the scene so that the readers see your characters in the scenes. Let the story unfold as it happens, whenever possible.

Smaller Things to Polish
Put

Put is another boring and vague verb. Avoid it. Consider the difference in strength between these two statements: *After the fight, Sam put the corsage in Ellie's refrigerator and left. After the fight, Sam crammed the corsage in Ellie's refrigerator and left.*

Got

The word *got* is the past tense and the past participle of *get*, and while nothing is wrong with using it, it's harsh-sounding, and it has endless meanings. Writers don't need to shun the word entirely, but creative writers prefer stronger verbs and verbs that do not lead to repetition. Instead of *Half the students got the flu*, consider *Half the students caught the flu.*

Sometimes when you avoid *got* you find your stronger verb also shortens the sentence. For example, instead of *Tom got down on his hands and knees behind the sofa*, choose *Tom crouched behind the sofa.*

Thought/felt/believed

Think, thought, feel, felt, believe, believed—all those words tell, rather than show. Choose other words that show, rather than tell.

> **Tells:** Jerry thought he saw movement behind the bushes.
> **Possible rewrite that shows:** A slight jiggle of the bushes grabbed Jerry's attention.

> **Tells:** After Betty lost her job, she felt depressed.
> **Possible rewrite that shows:** Betty awoke on schedule,

before the truth hit her again. She had nowhere to go. She fell back in bed, a cloud of doom closing in on her.

Tells: Barbara believed her husband was cheating on her.
Possible rewrite that shows: Barbara dialed the phone. When the private investigator answered, she stammered, "My husband is cheating on me. I need evidence."

Realized

Tells: Jean realized that Richard might be her long-lost brother.
Possible rewrite that shows: Jean looked into Richard's eyes, hazel like hers, and scanned his dimpled cheeks that looked like her sister's. She tilted her head. "Were you by any chance adopted?" she blurted.

Take, Took

Take and *took* do not always trigger an opportunity to write in style, but they do, if used in a weak manner. Examine each appearance in your manuscript and decide for yourself. Here are some examples and possible rewrites that show what happens when a stronger verb replaces *take* or *took*.

Weak: Sanford took the box to Marie.
Stronger (Depicts more visual aspects and action):
- Sanford dragged the box to Marie.
- Sanford tossed the box to Marie.
- Sanford carried the box to Marie.

- Sanford delivered the box to Marie.
- Sanford presented the box to Marie.

Contractions in Narrative

Contractions are one word created from two, with an apostrophe to show that something is missing, such as *isn't*, which is derived from combining *is* and *not*. Contractions most often include a verb, but not always. Because contractions usually contain weak verbs, I shall address them in this chapter.

Contractions have their place, especially in dialogue. People speak in contractions. That's a fact.

Don't use contractions in narrative, though, unless you're writing in an informal style, the way I've written this book. Most publishers prefer narrative to be formal, without contractions.

Example of narrative contraction: He'd buy an antique, if it struck his fancy.
Better: He would buy an antique, if it struck his fancy.
Even better: He bought antiques that struck his fancy.

Example of narrative contraction: She'd decided to ignore the phone.
Better: She had decided to ignore the phone.
Even better: She ignored the phone.

Thesaurus as a Sidekick

In case you have not discovered the thesaurus function on your computer, I'm here to tell you that it can be your buddy, when you're ready to write in style. It can also be your cruelest enemy, so use it with caution. The original thesaurus was a printed book that listed synonyms for most words. If a writer discovered he had overused *fall*, for example, he might open *Roget's Thesaurus* and find the following synonyms for *fall*: descend, stumble, succumb, decline, regress, occur, lower, totter, trip, plunge, keel, pitch, surrender, abate, decrease, diminish, relapse, recede, ebb, subside, befall, arrive, and so on. Not all the words have the same meaning, but they all can replace *fall* in certain usage.

Today we no longer have to open a book to find synonyms. Most of our computers have a thesaurus function. When you are ready to write in style and replace weak and vague verbs with stronger ones, use the thesaurus function on your computer. As you can see from the list above—which by the way is incomplete—a thesaurus is a great resource, but use it sensibly. Never choose a word that you would not use in conversation. If you do, the word will stand out like a pimple on prom night. Instead, let the words in your thesaurus trigger your natural memory.

Not every word has the same exact meaning, either, so as you look down the list of alternate words in your thesaurus, pick the one with the exact nuance you want.

The Find Frustration

Weak verbs do not have a standard structure, so running a single Find process will not locate all of them. Instead you have to run a Find process on quite a few weak verbs. See a suggested list below.

When you use your computer to search for words in the list below, examine the sentence and see if the word is a weak or vague verb in that sentence. Change the ones that help you write in style.

- Is, are, am, was, were, be, been, being
- Do
- Place
- Put
- Would
- Could
- Did
- Had, have, 've, 'd
- Got
- Feel, felt, think, thought, believe, believed
- Take, took
- Realize, realized

Exercises

Are you ready to put to the test the information I've given you? Good. Type the following sentences into your computer. Use the list above to find specific words. Mull over how you might rewrite the sentence better, and then compare your rewrites to mine. In creative writing you will not find absolutes, so your changes may be as good as or better than mine; they do not have to match mine. Here goes:

1. What she is planning is to redo her kitchen and place the refrigerator nearer to the counter, where she feels she will do most of her work.
2. Sara had put all her strength into taking the flowers to her ex-husband's new wife, who'd probably been in the wings during Sara's marriage.
3. Lee could hear the band as it was starting to put their instruments in tune.

4. When the package got to Elizabeth, she realized she'd made a mistake.

5. It took forever for the sun to rise, Susan thought.

6. There were times when he'd had enough, and he would yell to his neighbors to turn down their stereo.

7. Who'd have thought that the place would be so dark?

8. After Jim had proposed to Bonnie, he'd had second thoughts.

9. Karen lowered her limp grandchild and placed him gently into the crib blankets, believing he was asleep.

10. If I'd done the lottery yesterday with the same numbers I'd used today, I would've won.

Potential rewrites

1. She plans to renovate her kitchen and locate the refrigerator nearer to the counter, where she works most of the time.

2. Sara mustered all her strength to deliver the flowers to her ex-husband's new wife, a woman who probably lurked in the wings during Sara's marriage.

3. Lee heard the band tune up.

4. When Elizabeth received the package, she said, "I made a mistake."

5. The sun took forever to rise, in Susan's opinion.

6. At times he could not take the noise any longer and yelled at his neighbors to turn down their stereo.

7. Who would have predicted that the place would be so dark?

8. After Jim proposed to Bonnie, he rethought his decision.
9. Karen lowered her limp grandchild and nestled him into the crib blankets, believing he was asleep. (Remember, some words considered weak are not always avoidable!)
10. If I had entered the lottery yesterday with the same numbers I used today, I would have won.

Watch Out for Manu-slips!

Just for fun, here are a few typos, flaws, and other mistakes I've spotted in manuscripts as I edited. Many may have been attempts at writing stronger verbs. As you can see, not all rewrites work, so be careful when you rewrite.

- My anxious tears burst into the room. [Did the tears knock on the door first?]
- He made a fist and angrily shot his arm forward. [We did not know he had a gun.]
- His eyes turned guilty as they darted to the bruises on her arm. [Perhaps a set of contact lenses would have turned his eyes from guilty back to blue.]
- John's head snapped to the center aisle. [Ouch.]
- Laboring on this meticulous plan for over seven years, it's finally nearing completion. [As written *it* has been laboring.]
- When introduced to the class, dimples appeared near her smile. [Her dimples were introduced to the class?]
- Steven is tricked into making heroine deliveries.[He delivered female heroes, and for that reason the police arrested him?]

6

EXAMINING OTHER VERBAL FORMS

Writing is fun, especially when you are enjoying doing it, and it is keeping you entertained.

Above I've given you an acceptable sentence that complies with correct grammar and punctuation rules, but did you like it? Probably not. It comes across as sluggish, repetitive, and dull. I'll show you new ways to make your writing dash across the finish line, rather than stall before it reaches its mark.

We know that verbs are the gasoline that gives our sentences power, but like petroleum, verbs come in many forms. Which would you rather put into your engine, high-test gasoline or gloppy crude oil? As with engines, use refined fuel in your prose, and you'll write in style.

To make my point, let me repeat: *Writing is fun, especially when what you are enjoying doing it, and it is keeping you entertained.* In this sentence, you'll find four words that end in "ing": *writing, enjoying, doing,* and *keeping.* All four words originated as verbs—*write, enjoy, do,* and *keep*—but all are transformed into something weaker, something called a gerund, which takes an active verb and turns it into an inactive form: a noun. We won't worry about the technical terminology. All you have to remember is that you write in style when you avoid the "ing" trap.

Avoid the Ping

Forget that gerunds are nouns and participles are adjectives. Most people do not remember the difference, anyway. Both gerunds and participles end in "ing," though, so all you need to remember is Ping! Don't let your prose ping like an out-of-whack engine.

Words that end with "ing" drain the action out of the verb. The verb no longer has spunk. When you rely on too many "ing" words, the writing gets mired, and action stalls.

Painting is creative. The dancing was energetic. Traveling exhausted me. All these sentences rely on "ing" words and do not give a visual impression. Did you see any action? Nope, not at all. Editors hate "ing" words for those and other reasons.

Words like *painting*, *dancing*, and *traveling*, while still verbal forms, are no longer verbs, and they do not drive the sentence. Instead, sentences that use "ing" often must employ weak verbs to complete the sentence, usually some conjugation of *to be*, a static verb devoid of action. *Writing is fun.* See the weak verb, *is*? Those weak verbs add up quickly, and soon the writing looks like a grade-school writer reporting "What I did last summer."

Stylish writing shuns static verbs when possible and powers itself with verbs that move us, show us, and carry the story or information forward.

We already discussed linking verbs such as *is*, *are*, *was*, *were*, and other forms of *to be* in chapter five. Linking verbs join a noun idea with a description, but they don't take your sentence anywhere, as if you tried to tow a trailer without a vehicle.

Don't Let Your Participle Dangle

Words that end in "ing" set up sentences for failure or even ridicule, if you don't use extreme caution with them. We've all heard the term "dangling participle," but many of us don't understand it.

Most often, a dangling participle refers to an "ing" word without a proper modifier. When it hangs out by itself, it lends itself to improper interpretation, such as in this sentence from an unedited manuscript: *Having had two beers and an apple for breakfast, John's bladder alerted him that it needed relief.* On first read, the uninitiated may find the sentence acceptable, but a grammarian would see that it says that John's bladder had two beers and an apple for breakfast. The sentence never clearly states that John was the person who drank and ate those things. To repair, you might rewrite the sentence this way: *John drank two beers and ate an apple for breakfast, and his bladder alerted him that it needed relief.* In the rewrite, we see who consumed the less-than-glorious breakfast. Note that the rewrite relies on action verbs, *drank* and *ate*, whereas the original used *having* and *had*, which lack action and visual aspects.

Although you might think you would never leave your participles dangling, it happens all the time, and dangling participles will make you guffaw, once you spot them. You don't want people to laugh at your writing, except when you intend to entertain them.

Here's an even better example of a dangling participle: *Lifting her legs into the car, it took off down the road.* As written, the sentence says the car lifted her legs into itself. To correct it, write this: *She lifted her legs into the car, and it took off down the road.* In the rewrite, the "ing" word becomes a strong action verb, *lifted*.

Even More Dangling Things

Although dangling "ing" words are easier to spot with your computer Find program, they aren't the only things that can dangle and bring a smile to an editor. Any dangling modifier can do it. Examine this sentence from an unedited manuscript: *Cold and tired, his mind drifted back.* At first glance you might understand it, but a skilled editor would see that the sentence means that his mind was cold and tired, because nowhere in that sentence does it state otherwise. The modifiers *cold and tired* have nothing else to modify but *his mind,* and that's why editors call it a dangling modifier. To correct it, you might rewrite this way: *Because he was cold and tired, his mind drifted back.* Even better, write without a static verb: *Cold and tired, he let his mind drift back.* Notice how the rewrites add the pronoun *he* to indicate who is cold and tired, so that *cold* and *tired* logically modify *he.*

Ready to Write in Style?

Use my Find and Refine Method to find your "ing" words and examine them to see if you can turn them into action verbs. Type in the letters "ing" in your Find function. Each time the computer finds an "ing" word, think twice. First try to change the sentence to avoid "ing." If you decide you must leave the word in its "ing" form, be certain it correctly modifies a logical and nearby noun or pronoun. Also check for too many other "ing" forms nearby and reduce the repetition. Do everything you can to avoid duplication of any similar word or suffix nearby. In case you don't remember what a suffix is, it's an element added at the end of a word. In the words *laughing, hopelessly,* and *dancer,* the suffixes are "ing," "ly," and "er."

Dangling modifiers that do not incorporate "ing" don't stand out as easily. If you discover a way to find them on your computer, please let me know. Until then, you will become an expert at spotting dangling participles ("ing" words) with the help of the Find and Refine Method, and as a result, you may spot other dangling modifiers when they appear in your writing. You'll have a chance to do so in the following exercises and Manu-slips as well.

Type the sentences below into your computer. Apply my Find and Refine Method as described in chapter three. In the Find window, type in "ing." Examine each use of "ing" to determine if another word or a different structure would improve the sentence. Rewrite these sentences and compare your revisions to mine, that follow.

1. Dancing all night, the sun rose too early for the couple.
2. The terrier was playing with the bouncing ball and running after it, trying to catch it.
3. Michael stood six feet tall in his boots looking out at the horizon.
4. Millie scanned the clearing thinking anyone could walk up unnoticed.
5. Dressing in cowboy outfits, the brass belt buckles often chafed his stomach.
6. While looking for help, Mark kept snagging his skin on brambles.
7. Exhaling, Harriett's forehead relaxed.
8. Fluttering leaves were falling to the darkening deck.
9. Donald was watching the UFO shoot into the air before going inside to call the police.

10. Laughing, John said, "I was waiting for the dancing girls."

Possible rewrites:

1. The couple danced all night, and the sun rose too early for them.
2. The terrier played with the bouncing ball and ran after it, in an attempt to catch it.
3. Michael, who stood six feet tall in his boots, looked out at the horizon.
4. Millie scanned the clearing. "Anyone could walk up unnoticed," she remarked.
5. When he dressed in cowboy outfits, the brass belt buckles often chafed his stomach.
6. Mark stumbled through the woods to get help, and the brambles snagged and ripped at his skin.
7. Harriett exhaled, and her forehead relaxed.
8. Leaves fluttered to the deck that grew darker by the minute.
9. Donald watched the UFO shoot into the air before he ran inside to call the police.
10. John laughed. "I was waiting for the dancing girls."

Slip on These Manu-slips for a Smile

I hope these Manu-slips that feature gerunds, dangling participles, and missing modifiers make you smile and teach you a little along the way, as well.

- Standing under the yellow porch light of Marsha's parents' house, John's kiss was polite and wholesome.

[As written, John's kiss stood under the light. To repair, you might rewrite the sentence this way: *While John and Marsha stood under the yellow porch light of Marsha's parent's house, his kiss was polite and wholesome.*]

- Walking quickly to avoid the breezy subzero weather, her hands were in the pockets of her overcoat. [To keep her hands from walking, I'd rewrite it this way: *She walked quickly to avoid the breezy subzero weather, her hands in the pockets of her overcoat.*]

- Sweating slightly in mink and sable, their hair fluttered in the evening breeze. [To stop their hair from sweating: *The pair sweated a little in their mink and sable coats, and their hair fluttered in the evening breeze.*]

- While conducting the search inside the house, storm clouds had gathered. [To keep the clouds from searching the house, perhaps rewrite this way: *While the police conducted the search inside the house, storm clouds gathered outside.*]

- Clinging to the counter, his heart pounded in his ears. [Please destroy the vision of his heart clinging to the counter. Consider this rewrite: *He clung to the counter, and his heart pounded in his ears.*]

- Frail but physically healthy in all respects, early observers took an interest, recorded that the infant never uttered so much as a whimper. [As written, the observers were frail, although the author intended to mean the baby was frail. The sentence needs to be rewritten to say that observers of the infant recorded that although he was frail, he was physically healthy in all respects.]

- Although granted a pardon moments before execution, the pilot's instincts took over. [The pilot's instincts were granted a pardon, as written. Rewrite, possibly this way: *Although the pilot was granted a pardon moments before his execution, his instincts took over.*]

- More nights than he could remember were spent cramming for exams pumped up with amphetamines. [His exams were pumped with speed, huh? To clarify and avoid passive voice, consider this revamp: *He spent more nights than he could remember cramming for exams while pumped up with amphetamines.*]

- Smiling, her sparkling white teeth contrasted with her deep olive skin. [How would you rewrite it to keep her teeth from smiling?]

7

ADJUST THE LEVEL OF ADJECTIVES

Adjectives—words that describe nouns or pronouns—add polish and shine to descriptions. Instead of describing any tree, when we add an adjective, we can make readers imagine a tall tree, a broad tree, a leafless tree, a maple tree, or a pine tree.

Adjectives Add Definition and Clarity

Let's think of adjectives as the paint job on an automotive body. Paint is not essential to the operation of the vehicle, but when applied properly, it makes the car more attractive. If smeared on, though, the paint becomes an eyesore.

Our high-school teachers told us adjectives add exactness to writing, but many writers go to extremes with them.

Like high-quality paint, good adjectives appeal to the senses. Few sentences need adjectives, but a good adjective helps readers visualize the exact subject. Smudge on too many adjectives, and you might as well park your manuscript in a bottom drawer and forget it.

Don't give up, though. You'll rescue the manuscript when you write in style.

Let's scrutinize adjectives. Adjectives describe—or modify—nouns and pronouns, as in the following example: *Jessica wore a short skirt.* By itself, *Jessica wore a skirt* might be enough to answer a simple question, such as "What did Jessica wear to work?" Beyond that, the readers do not learn much. Without the adjective (*short*), the sentence gives little visual information. When you add a single adjective, *short,* the mind conjures up a vision, perhaps of her legs inappropriately displayed at the office. Good writing stays as visual as possible, and each word has a reason for existing. One adjective adds an acceptable visual element to the sentence and implants an image in the minds of readers. The information sets the stage for events that follow.

More Is Rarely Better

If good writing relies on visual images, why not go all out? The result might be something like this sentence: *Jessica wore a short, brown, wool-knit skirt.* Although the revision has visual aspects, they are painted on too thick. Most readers hold one image at a time in their minds. If all that information is important, let it come out gradually, rather than in a string, and use action.

Jessica slid her short skirt up and settled into the chair across from the president. She looked down at the brown fabric and picked lint off the wool knit.

In the two-sentence example, readers see action. They get the picture, and they get it one piece at a time, as the scene plays out. You've given readers all the same information, but you haven't slathered it on in one thick stroke.

Examine the following: *A lanky black antique German cuckoo clock sat in one corner.* English teachers would say the sentence follows the rules of grammar, but a good editor would point to the bulky layer of adjectives—*lanky, black, antique, German,* and *cuckoo*—and say, "Yuck!" Editors call layered adjectives "adjective strings," and to illustrate their ineffectiveness, we number the adjectives. One adjective is good, but add another adjective, and you reduce the effectiveness by half. We illustrate the equation this way: $1 + 2 = \frac{1}{2}$. More than two adjectives in a row, and the description loses even more impact. We might number the adjectives to show the magnitude of their lost effectiveness. The equation might look like: $1 + 2 + 3 = 0$. In the sample above, the sentence might be shown this way:

$$1 + 2 + 3 + 4 + 5 = 0$$

A lanky black antique German cuckoo clock sat in one corner.

To repair an adjective string, limit adjectives to one or two per noun. One is better than two. Descriptions work best when threaded through action and dialogue.

Let's say you are introducing a character in a novel or writing a personality profile for a magazine. Before you knew how to write in style, you might have written this example: *Deborah was a tall, slender blonde wearing a blue pinstriped tailored business suit.*

Now that you know how to write in style, you might instead write: *Deborah, a tall blonde, wore a tailored suit in a blue that matched her eyes.*

Such a description puts readers into the room with the subject. When readers feel involved in a story, they get hooked. Show, rather than tell the story, and sprinkle adjectives a little at a time. In the process, you win over readers and editors alike, whether you're writing nonfiction or fiction, and you've written in style.

Other Adjective Warnings

Just as strings of adjective layer on the descriptions too thick and kill the pace of a paragraph, too many adjectives overall can kill the whole piece. Be careful not to modify too many nouns with adjectives. Any repeated pattern grows boring to readers, and the wordiness kills the pace. Note the following excerpt from an unpolished manuscript. Almost every noun has an adjective in this sample:

> A big gust sent a blizzard of pink cherry blossoms swirling across the yard. Gray tree branches held out swollen buds. The squealing protest of worn brakes caught my attention. A black Cavalier sedan pulled onto the berm. From the driver's side leaped a gaunt man in a dull gray suit, his face marred by savage scars.

The paragraphs have no technical errors, but the style—the pattern of almost every noun preceded by one or two adjectives—creates a singsong effect that rocks readers to sleep. The sample sports fifteen nouns and fifteen adjectives. Change sentence structure, sentence length, and word choices often, to keep readers alert and entertained.

How would you rewrite those sentences to get much of the same information across without so many adjectives? You might want to spread the information around in other places, instead of jamming it all so close together.

Another Reason to Reconsider Adjectives

Adjectives give readers information, but sometimes teasing them with fewer details entices them into reading more.

Examine any sentence that contains more than one adjective. *The dog had a full, thick coat* may sound fine, but either adjective (*full* or *thick*) would say the same thing, without flab. Employ only one adjective at a time: *The dog had a full coat. The dog had a thick coat.* Either revision works better than the original. An even better change would show the dog in action, rather than telling about it in a static way: *The dog's thick coat swayed when he trotted across the carpet.*

Fiction and creative nonfiction offer opportunities for description and therefore call for more adjectives than business writing. No matter what the project, remember to use adjectives wisely. Insert them one at a time, preferably within action. Whenever you introduce a character and want to describe him, her, or it, consider every adjective. Instead of adjectives that tell, use scenes that show the true character of the individual you want readers to get to know.

Assemble Characters from Their Parts in the Story

Don't stop dialogue and action to give a narrative description of any of the characters. Here's an example of poor narrative description:

> Amanda Minnelli had long legs, long eyelashes, and a short skirt. Her hair was cut in a pageboy, and the ends were barely touching her cheeks. She had on a red blouse that was so small that her midriff appeared between it and the leather skirt that was hemmed at her thighs. She was pretty, and she knew it.

Notice that the narrative description relies on static linking verbs: *had, was, were,* and *appeared* (See chapter five for more on linking verbs). Linking verbs tell, rather than show, and good writers show, rather than tell a story.

How can you develop well-rounded, interesting characters? How can you show character description, rather than tell it? Instead of relying only on adjectives, develop the characters bit by bit, every time they appear in the manuscript. Below are more creative ways to keep your characters interesting while you write in style.

Physical Descriptions Add Little

Let's revisit the earlier description:

> Amanda Minnelli had long legs, long eyelashes, and a short skirt. Her hair was cut in a pageboy, and the ends were barely touching her cheeks. She had on a red blouse that was so small that her midriff appeared between it and the leather skirt that was hemmed at her thighs. She was pretty, and she knew it.

If we polished it into a form that shows rather than tells what the character looks like, it might come out like this:

> With long legs, Amanda Minnelli strode up to the judge and batted her long eyelashes. She patted her leather miniskirt, as if to straighten it, and her pageboy hair swished, the ends barely touching her cheeks. She stood erect, as if to ensure the judge noticed her midriff and belly peeking out between her red blouse and leather skirt hemmed at her thighs. She looked up at the judge through her lashes and flashed him a smile that displayed her deepest dimple.

Action verbs such as *strode, batted, patted, swished, stood, noticed, hemmed, looked, flashed,* and *displayed* replaced the static verbs—*had, was, were,* and *appeared.* Visualize the difference. Close your eyes and say, *"had, was, were,* and *appeared."* Does any image of movement come to mind? Does any image at all come to mind? Next close your eyes and say, *"strode, batted, patted, swished, stood, noticed, hemmed, looked, flashed,* and *displayed."* Notice the difference? With the second list, you picture action.

How would you rewrite the first description? I'll bet you can rewrite it in style even better than I did.

You might be happy enough with the second version, but keep in mind that the physical description of a character is the weakest piece of information you can give a reader. To develop characters and make them three-dimensional, do more than describe them. You must assemble them.

Let Characters Grow With the Story

Every time characters appear "on stage," let their actions and speech reveal their motives, background, style, and backgrounds.

Use Dialogue

When your characters speak among themselves, what do they say about their own preferences, prejudices, dreams, and goals? What they say, how they say it, and even how much they talk informs readers about your characters without your having to write narrative that tells.

Each character should have an individual style of speech. The less-educated may use poor grammar or wrong word choices, such as saying "prostrate cancer" instead of "prostate cancer." Professorial types may speak in stilted terms, such as "I shall endeavor to see that the job is completed" instead of "I'll see the job gets done." Here are some examples of dialogue between two characters. What do you learn about each?

"Hey, I want a pack of them green cigarettes."

"Pardon me, but do you mean you want the cigarettes in the green package, or are you saying you want the green cigarettes themselves?"

"Green cigs? I ain't never seen no green smokes. I'm talking about them in the green pack.

"Well, then, you mean these, yes? That will be five dollars, please."

"Five bucks? Are you trying to rip me off?"

"My dear sir, if you wanted the green ones, the Turkish cigarettes, you would pay eight dollars and fifty cents a pack. Your brand, sir, costs a pittance, in comparison."

Although the above dialogue lacks visual clues, narrative, action, or attributions (I call such a conversation "Dialogue in a Vacuum" or "Talking Heads"), I used the example to make a point. You can show much about the characters by their word choices, reactions, knowledge, attitudes, and preferences.

As you write, all your characters should reveal something of themselves through their manner of speech. Avoid writing in dialects, however. Dialect is difficult to write well and frustrating to read. Never alienate readers.

Use Body Language

When you show what your characters do, you communicate a great deal to your readers. When Bianca touches her lips often, she could be telling a lie or be hesitant to speak. When Joe crosses his arms when someone else speaks, Joe could be closed to what the other person is saying. If Georgina crosses her arms while she herself speaks, she may be withholding information.

People do many things that reveal nonverbal communication. When you add shrugs, raised eyebrows, frowns, pencil tapping, chin touching, steepled fingers, and other body language, you show a little insight into the character. Use your imagination. Watch real people and take notes about body language. Folks do all sorts of fascinating things when they talk. They rock on their heels, shift their weight, wink, lean back in seats, pick their nails, brush back their hair, scratch (sometimes in inappropriate places), glance at their cell phones, and do all manner of other things. Add those visual images to your fiction or nonfiction manuscript, and your character grows in strength for your readers.

In manuscripts I edit, too often the dialogue-related action is limited to smiles, grins, laughs, and frowns. Make your characters show their personalities through a wide variety of their bodily actions. Learn about body language, which goes far beyond the obvious. Here's an interesting challenge: Take paper and a pen to several places, such as a mall, a fine restaurant, a coffee shop, a fast-food joint, a poetry reading, a liquor store, a supermarket, a pet store, a park, a place of worship, or a business meeting. Pay close attention to what others do with their bodies as they speak to you or to others and even when they don't speak. Observe carefully. Write notes. Question everything. Determine if body language changes from setting to setting. Decide what people mean by their physical actions.

Do you know what's going on when someone leans back and put his hands behind his head? The action might mean the person feels in charge, on top. It can also be the gesture of someone trying to establish dominance. Only from the situation and dialogue can a person ascertain the difference, and that's where your skills as a writer come in.

If your boss stormed into your office, slammed the door, plopped down across from you, propped his feet up on your desk, leaned back in his chair, and laced his fingers behind his head, what might that mean? A boss who feels threatened by you might display such behavior and body language while chastising you. A friend might display similar body language before bragging about an accomplishment. Something is definitely taking place in the power department. Embed clues in the body language of characters.

In *The Joy Luck Club*, Amy Tan wrote this revealing passage that uses body language and reveals much about her Asian mother's feelings at the time:

> "That cat gone! Disappear!" She threw her hands in the air and smiled, looking pleased for a moment before the scowl came back.

Make notes while you observe people when they talk, watch, or listen. Read a book on body language. Add body language to your writing to reveal your characters' thoughts, feelings, and attitudes, and you write in style.

Use Names

Select last names that reflect ethnic backgrounds. What comes to mind with each of the following last names: Montoya, Schwartz, Lorinski, Jiménez, and Bonnano? What if all the names were changed to Brown, Jones, Smith, James, and Barnes? The characters lose everything, don't they?

Use first names that reflect family background and views. For example, if the family is Jewish, choose traditional given names, such as Ruth, Sam, Joseph, or Susan. If the family is southern, consider names such as Hope, Mary Josephine, Bubba, or Junior. Do these names sound stereotypical? Perhaps they are, but some things are a fact of life. Don't buck a trend; use it in your favor, unless you have a distinct reason for going against tradition.

To take names a step further, show how the characters in your stories react to their names and nicknames. Perhaps Hope finds her name embarrassing, or maybe she's depressed about it. Marilyn Josephine might find her name complicated and ask friends to call her Mare. Individual reactions to names can reveal something deep within a character's psyche.

Does Everyone Need a Name?

Not every character in a manuscript deserves a name, and minor characters should not have viewpoints, either. For example, if a doorman greets a visitor to an apartment building, do readers need the doorman's name or what the doorman thought of the visitor? If characters appear only once or twice in the manuscript, don't give their names unless you must, to move the story forward. For example, if a visitor calls the doorman by name, readers get the message that the visitor often passes through. If the doorman plays a major part in the story, though, readers should know his first and last name and may even be allowed into his point of view.

Names—especially first and last names together—give a subtle message to readers that the character is going to be important to the story. When you name every character, including minor ones, you create a long list of names readers think they must remember, when all they may need to remember is a small piece of information, such as the apartment has a doorman.

Consistency Adds Clarity

When a major character appears for the first time, give the character's first and last name right away. From that point on, call the character by either the first name or last name, but not the first name sometimes and the last name at other times. In other words, do not call a character Buddy Carter in one place, Bud in another, and Carter in yet another. I recommend using first names after the first mention, because two or more characters that are related may have the same last name. Oh, and in the narrative, never use courtesy titles such as Mr. or Mrs.

Use Real People

Why try to manufacture characters, when real ones abound? To build stimulating literary characters, rely on what you know about real people. Be certain, however, to change your character enough so Uncle Fred will not recognize himself as the alcoholic who abandoned his children, and Mrs. Peabody won't know she is the history teacher who gave mixed signals to her students. Change names, descriptions, careers, and much more, to avoid legal liability.

In my seminar called Rev Up Your IQ (Imagination Quotient), I give an exercise during which the participants study several other people in a circle. Each person then writes a composite character with traits from all those people. As participants read what they've put together, each writer's creation sounds genuine, yet no two are alike, even when they had looked at the same group of human beings. If you create composite characters, you'll people your stories with authentic characters without leaving yourself open to litigation.

Choose an Educational Background

Even if you never share all the information about the characters, as the writer, you should know all about the people who live in your manuscript. To help with that knowledge, choose the types and levels of schools the character attended. A person with a law degree talks, writes, and speaks in a way that differs from one who did not finish high school. Keep educational backgrounds in mind as you write dialogue.

Use Setting

A character's birthplace or chosen environment can reveal his or her social status and attitudes. Enrich characters through their surroundings by putting the characters in their old neighborhoods or among siblings or parents in a flashback. Reveal information about the places they choose to live as adults and how those settings contrast with or reflect what the characters learned and did in childhood. Background influences characters' choices of clothing as well as their tastes in music, literature, and other activities.

What background might influence a grown person to enjoy sitting on the front porch in a rocking chair? You may not find someone who grew up in inner city New York relaxing in a porch rocker as an adult. You might find her leaning out a window of a stoop, though. Would someone who grew up on a farm lean out a window to watch traffic in later life? Maybe not. Be sure your characters feel authentic in their settings and with their histories.

What kind of background would you expect from someone who plays polo? How about someone who uses heroin? What sort of background might lead to an adult who abuses a spouse?

Build those backgrounds into your story, and you build believable characters and write in style.

Use the Character Trait Chart

To flesh out the significant characters in a novel, use the Character Trait Chart in the back of this book. If you have five major characters, make five copies of the chart and fill one out for each. You may never need all the information on the chart, but filling in the details allows you to see your character as a whole person. As a result you will have an easier time keeping that person in character as you write your manuscript.

You may want to use a photograph of a real person as part of the chart. If you are working in fiction, you may draw a composite to create a character or cut a picture out of a magazine. Use anything that assists your visualization of the character while you write

I Digressed

Let's not forget the main subject, though: adjectives. I explained all the information on building characters, so you can see the weakness of stringing adjectives together to describe a character, compared to all the strong ways to describe characters through the way they live and the things they do and say.

You now know not to use too many adjectives when you describe characters. Remember to avoid the same pitfall when you describe settings. Here are some tips to help you be even more descriptive when grounding your scenes in a good setting.

Settings

Like descriptions of characters, descriptions of surroundings also work best in small doses. Strong writers describe scenes without overusing adjectives and without narrative that detracts from the action. Readers do need a setting, especially in fiction and creative nonfiction, to help them visualize the scene, but for maximum effect, show the setting amid action and dialogue.

Examine the following hypothetical description:

> The Anglican Church was set far back from the street. It looked sad and small, compared to other churches in the city. Its clapboard exterior was painted white, and the marquee out front listed the Bible verse for the week, along with the name of the minister. Evelyn feared the old, thin front steps might not hold her hefty weight.

How would you rewrite the description to make it show, rather than tell the setting? Here's one way:

> Mary drove past several sprawling churches before she finally spotted the Anglican Church marquee in front of a modest building. After she parked by the sign that listed the minister's name and a Bible verse, Evelyn walked along the sidewalk to reach the aging steps. She put one elephantine foot on the wood, testing its strength, and steadied her heft with a hand on the white clapboard.

By interspersing adjectives amid action, the story continues, yet it remains visual. Readers can imagine the setting.

Notice I did not include *sad* in the second description. Read on, to learn why.

Not All Adjectives Are Equal

Like paint, the quality of adjectives differs. Pick a cheap paint, and the primer shows through. Pick a weak adjective, an abstract one instead of a concrete one, and the author's voice bleeds through. When an author's opinion shows through the writing, editors refer to the phenomenon as "editorializing" or "author intrusion." In an essay, readers expect to hear the author's opinion. In other writing, though, except for manuscripts written in first person, editors advise against author intrusion. *Sad*, as it appears above, was the opinion of the author. It did not help readers visualize the church, so it needed to be deleted.

The following passage, full of some author's opinion, would be acceptable and go unnoticed in most essays:

> The way America treats its homeless is atrocious. Everywhere you turn, pitiful people roam the streets begging for a handout, anything to fuel their empty stomachs or drug habits one more day.

In a novel, though, unless written as dialogue, the passage reveals the author's opinion. It does not show; it tells, and it uses some abstract adjectives to do so. Notice the terms *atrocious* and *pitiful*, which are opinions, abstract adjectives, and not concrete descriptions.

Remember this: abstract adjectives give opinions; concrete ones give descriptions. Abstract adjectives involve ideas, the invisible; concrete adjectives are visible, or at least tangible.

Let's return to the same passage about homeless Americans. Written in style, it might look this way:

> As Jeremy drove down the city streets, he saw ragged people everywhere. Some dug in trash cans; others held signs on their laps while they sat on street corners. Many stepped up to his car and begged for change, anything to fuel their empty stomachs or drug habits one more day. "That's atrocious," he mumbled. "We can put a man on the moon, but we can't feed our own people."

The second version attributes the thoughts to a character, rather than the author, and it keeps the scene visual.

As you can see, dialogue and quotations may use abstract adjectives, because they are attributable to a person other than the author, but in narrative, avoid abstract adjectives such as these: *awesome, pretty, handsome, nice, sexy, beautiful, horrible, ugly, expensive,* and *generous*. The list could go on, but you get the idea. Instead of abstract adjectives, use concrete ones to describe the person, place, or thing, and let readers form their own opinions.

Concrete adjectives—adjectives that appeal to the sense of smell, taste, touch, sight or hearing—usually represent better choices than abstract adjectives. As an example, let's say you want readers to know a woman is pretty. Which of the following examples would be preferable? *Sally was pretty. Sally's auburn hair fell in ringlets beside her high cheekbones.*

You would choose the second example, of course, because it allows readers to visualize Sally and decide for themselves that she is pretty. Number one does not give any concrete information that allows readers to imagine how Sally looks.

Here's another one. How would you say that a character was sexy? A concrete description might come out like this: *When she slid one silk-stockinged leg over the other, her skirt raised, revealing a flawless thigh.* The concrete descriptions—the visual ones—show, rather than tell, and readers experience the scene for themselves.

Comma "Rules" Often Are Only Style Guidelines

Although adjectives differ too much to find them with one swift computer search, one shortcut is to use the Find and Refine Method to find commas and check to see if they indicate excessive use of adjectives. Before you set your computer to check for commas, let me give you a few other opportunities for improvement that may also arise while you look for commas.

Gather a roomful of writers, and you'll get varying but convincing reasons regarding when and where to put commas. Most writers think the use of commas follows immutable rules. Wrong. The use of commas is dictated not by rule, but by style.

Chapter two discusses style guides and their differences more thoroughly, but let me give you a few reminders. Most periodicals—newspapers, newsletters, and magazines—adhere to Associated Press style. AP style does not put a comma before *and* in a series, as in the following example: *The caterer will serve hot dogs, baked beans and ice cream.* If you write articles, do not use a comma before *and* in a series.

If you are writing a novel or nonfiction book, chances are good that your publisher prefers Chicago style, which calls for commas before *and* or *or* in a series, so the sentence would be as follows: *The caterer will serve hot dogs, baked beans, and ice cream.*

Writing a memo? Business style shuns the extra comma as well, so you would write *The caterer will serve hot dogs, baked beans and ice cream.*

Before you search for commas to find descriptive words and paragraphs to revamp and improve, decide which style you need to use (remember, most book publishers prefer Chicago style), and add or delete commas to fit the style you want to follow. Be consistent. More than anything, style guides promote uniformity.

Length Matters

While you search for commas, also pay attention to see if your commas point out sentences that are too long. Lengthy sentences grow clumsy and difficult to understand. They often confuse readers. Never risk losing the reader.

Instead of being powerful, wordy sentences lose their impact. Keep sentences unencumbered.

How long is too long? Only you can tell. While conventional wisdom says that sentences grow unwieldy when they contain more than ten words, if you use too many short sentences, the writing gets choppy. Too many elongated ones, though, will kill the pace and lose readers. An occasional pregnant sentence changes the pace, but editors advise writers to use only a few, here and there. Common sense says that sentences that contain twenty words are too long, yet I've seen sentences as long as forty-two words. Many long sentences fail when they cram too much information into one statement. For example, look at the following sentence from an unedited manuscript:

The subtle flattery and the thought of playing again a sport that she had enjoyed physically and with some success, after all she had played in the state champion doubles while in high school and had reached the quarter final in singles competition, elicited a favorable reaction, quickly tempered with an almost latent reservation and restraint.

At what point did you get lost? The writer tried to convey too many pieces of information at one time and did it poorly. If you have to gasp for air when you read your own sentence out loud, I guarantee you that it's too long and too complicated. A few dashes in the sentence above might have aided reader comprehension, but break the information into several sentences and cut out the flab, and the result might be this:

His flattery made her feel good. She had played in the state champion doubles in high school and had reached the quarter final in singles competition, so the thought of playing again elicited a favorable reaction. She quickly restrained herself, however.

Even better might be a total rewrite that shows, and it might go like this:

When Joe suggested playing tennis, she jumped from her seat. "Oh, yes! I'd love it! I used to play doubles in high school." She sat back down. "That is, I guess I could still play, if I tried."

Here's an example of another long sentence that puts together too many ideas. It, as do most long sentences, lends itself to breaking into smaller segments:

Mary liked fresh egg bagels, and she often drove fourteen long miles down the highway from her house to buy the unique ones sold at the bakery near the river in the middle of town.

A possible rewrite might go like this:

Mary liked egg bagels and often drove fourteen miles to buy fresh ones. Her favorite bakery sat next to the river in the middle of town.

Read on for other things to consider, when your computer finds a comma for you.

Items in a List Share Common Modifiers

If modifiers such as prepositions, adjectives, adverbs, or articles precede objects in a list, they apply to all items. Let's examine this sentence: *John's gaze took in Barbara's slender waist, hips, thighs, ankles, and gold shoes.* In that example, *slender* modifies all the nouns that follow, which means John looked at Barbara's slender waist, slender hips, slender thighs, slender ankles, and slender gold shoes. If only the waist was slender, rewrite the sentence in one way or another. Sometimes changing the order can help. *John's gaze took in Barbara's ankles, thighs, hips, slender waist, and gold shoes.* You can also add a word to separate the items and clarify which adjective modifies which item. *John's gaze took in Barbara's slender waist as well as her hips, thighs, ankles, and gold shoes.* In either rewrite, *slender* modifies only the intended word.

Hyphen Help

I have already made the point that one strong adjective beats two. Some overblown adjectives are hyphenated, such as the ones in this example: *Manny's blue-black hair looked darker under his snow-white hat.*

As with verbs, strong adjectives are better than weak ones. Let me remind you again never to ignore the power of the thesaurus. A word of warning, though: If you're not sure of the implications of a word you select from the thesaurus, don't use it, or if you feel you must use it, at least look it up in the dictionary to be certain it reflects the nuance you intended to portray. Now, on to hyphen-linked adjectives, which often represent weak adjectives.

Wherever you have hyphenated adjectives, they signal the opportunity to find one strong one that says the same thing, but even better. Examine every hyphenated adjective in your text, and search for one strong word that describes the noun better. Instead of *thick-waisted*, consider using *stout*. Instead of *odd-looking*, consider a more definite description, such as this: *His ears stuck out, and his cheeks bore freckles the size of poker chips.*

As you locate hyphenated adjectives in your work, check a thesaurus for alternate descriptions. Look for ways to be original, and always avoid unintentional repetition.

To reduce your adjectives, use the Find and Refine Method to locate hyphens. Although a search for hyphens won't catch all your adjectives, it will catch some of the overblown ones. Let me explain a little more about hyphens. You may decide to eliminate most compound adjectives, but first you need to understand when to use them.

Hyphens join words. Hyphens string together compound adjectives (*a raven-haired boy, his ten-year-old sister*) to avoid ambiguity or form a single idea from two or more words.

Some hyphenated adjectives would be better as one word or the other. *A wood-slatted house* might become *a wooden house*. You can eliminate other hyphenated adjectives through changing the order of the sentence. *A red-dotted dress* might change to *a dress with red dots*. You may exchange some hyphenated adjectives for one word that is better than two or more. For example, *a blue-green dress* might change to *an aquamarine dress*. You can eliminate some words, such as *looking*. *An old-looking building sat on the lot* can be *An old building sat on the lot*.

I also see dozens of words hyphenated that should be one word. For example, *lunch-time crowd* should be *lunchtime crowd*. *On-board radio* should be *onboard radio*. Some spelling and grammar checkers may catch an occasional error such as those two, but because each word can stand alone, many computer spell-checkers will miss them. For example, as I write, the Microsoft Word version I use accepts both *spell-checker* and *spellchecker*. Chicago style calls for the *Merriam-Webster* version, though, which would have the hyphen, *spell-checker*.

When in question, look up both versions in Merriam-Webster to see which version is preferred, and note that sometimes the hyphen applies to one definition, yet the word spelled without a hyphen refers to a different definition.

Because spell-checkers are inconsistent in their ability to pick up two words that should be one, hyphen errors constitute one of the prevalent errors I correct in manuscripts. I could list hundreds of words I've seen incorrectly hyphenated or written as two words, including *lighthearted, foghorn, overripe, afterthought, straightforward, clockwork,* and *painkiller*.

English changes. Keep up with it. My father, who was born in the early 1900s, used *to-day* as a hyphenated word, for example, but that form fell out of favor years ago.

Look up all questionable hyphenated words. If you sense you have often seen the same two words together, the two words might be one or might be hyphenated. If you don't want to use the recommended *Merriam-Webster*, at least type the word as one and see if your spell-checker accepts it that way. I know extra checking means extra thinking and extra work, but the result is a manuscript written in style.

Insider Secret

Instead of relying on your spell-checker to tell you when to hyphenate, here's a secret that will help. If you cannot use one word or the other alone to describe the noun, hyphenate the words to create a one-word adjective. For example, if you could not decide whether to write *ten-foot pole* or *ten foot pole*, stop and think for a moment. *Ten pole* would be incorrect, as would *foot pole*. A hyphen would be appropriate in this case, to ensure everyone knows the pole was ten feet long. Notice when written as *ten feet long*, it needs no hyphen, because *ten* modifies only *feet*, in the second version.

After you have used the Find and Refine Method on commas, run one for hyphens. You may eliminate even more adjective strings and find ways to make more of your sentences stronger.

In this chapter you've learned that commas and hyphens often lead to opportunities to write clearer, stronger, and better. You've learned how to use adjectives sparingly and to reveal character in ways other than describing them physically.

Roll Up Your Sleeves and Write in Style

Let's get out that polishing cloth and put a high shine on your own work. Practice with the following sentences and see how your changes compare to the possible solutions. Remember that the primary purpose for these exercises is not to teach grammar and punctuation. Instead you have an opportunity to turn ragged prose into revved-up writing. Perform whatever maintenance you'd like, to make each sentence better than the original.

Use the Find and Refine Method. Type in the examples and run a Find on commas and make any changes you see fit. Next run a Find on hyphens and add the finishing touches to your changes. As you rewrite the sentences, use your head. Be creative, be visual, and be concise. When you have finished, compare your revisions to mine. Your adaptation might be even better than mine. I hope so.

1. The tall blonde wore a large, bright-red scarf on her scrawny neck.
2. Marsh grass is tall, thin, green, and has sharp edges that cut.
3. Harry always carried a velvet hat, coat, and cane, and he was a funny man.
4. Margaret plays a beat-up, brown Martin guitar with a small, round plug for the amplifier attached to the side.
5. The mountain trail leads through sparse, gnarled evergreen trees.
6. Silver star-shaped decorations hung from every branch of the sorry-looking Christmas tree.
7. Khaki-colored Army trucks streamed into town filled with exhausted, solemn soldiers.
8. The boy's book bag was brown, had five zippers and shoulder straps, and he filled it with smooth, round river rocks.

9. The recently elected heavy-set mayor rambled on and on, but despite his fancy-sounding expressions, he never said anything important, essential or significant.

10. Mornings in Bermuda are blue and beautiful, and the natives have a joke that they go out before daybreak to paint the sky and ocean blue.

Possible rewrites:

1. The scarlet scarf dwarfed the tall blonde's anorexic neck.

2. John maneuvered through the marsh grass with caution. The sharp edges of the tall greenery could slice into his legs.

3. Harry, an easygoing man, made everyone laugh. He always carried a cane, a velvet coat, and matching hat.

4. Margaret reaches into the case and lifts out a guitar. When the lights get brighter, they highlight the scars on its brown surface. On one side of the Martin, she attaches her amplifier cord to a small plug.

5. Gnarled evergreens dot the mountain trail.

6. Silver stars hung from every branch of the scraggly Christmas tree.

7. Khaki Army trucks filled with drooping soldiers streamed into town.

8. The boy unzipped all five compartments of his book bag and filled every one with rocks worn smooth by the river. He hefted the weight of the brown carryall and slipped his arms into the shoulder straps.

9. The new mayor reached down and pulled his trousers up over his paunch. "In view of the recent circumstances . . ." He cleared his throat. "In light of the situation, uh . . ."His gaze searched the crowd. "I'd like to say that the appropriate departments are looking into the matter, and a full report will be forthcoming." (By the way, did you notice that *heavy-set* should be one word, *heavyset*? Maybe not, though, because my rewrite deleted the word.)

10. Bermudans joke that they go out every morning before daybreak to paint the sky and water a deep blue.

Watch Out for Manu-slips!

Okay, enough of the hard work. Just for fun, here are a few typos, flaws, or other mistakes I've spotted in manuscripts I edited. You may choose to rewrite them or simply enjoy them.

- Relaxation removes pressures, tensions, a wish to do an even better job for the bosses who provided the vacation. [If relaxation removes a wish to do a better job for your boss, why would your boss want you to relax?]
- She ordered flounder stuffed with crabmeat and salad. [I'd rather have my salad outside the flounder, wouldn't you?]
- We talked about picking blackberries and rattlesnakes in the bushes while picking blackberries. [Where would you prefer to pick rattlesnakes?]
- He noticed a blond woman with a funny nose, unruly hair, thick makeup, and big breasts sitting at the bar. [Big breasts sitting at a bar will certainly get noticed.]

- "Think there's a possibility we could chat?" he crooned with a warm, bubbly smile that extended from his mouth all the way up to his wide-set, intense velvet brown eyes. [How could he see, with all those bubbles in his velvet eyes?]
- The nuns taught us games that were highly competitive, but with good sportsmanship, tap dancing, and gave recitals. [I wish the nuns had taught them how to write sentences with parallel elements.]
- He watched the Indians with their glistening copper-colored bodies and long, straight black hair wrestling alligators. [Their hair had to be strong, to wrestle alligators.]

AND ANOTHER THING: SEAT CONJUNCTIONS PROPERLY

C lients have asked me what's so wrong with starting an occasional sentence with *and, but, or, so, yet,* or *however.* They point out best-selling books and articles that use conjunctions to open sentences.

True, English changes constantly. One day, perhaps, even *ain't* will be accepted in formal English, as will other words to which scholars of today turn up their editorial noses. I agree that usage does eventually bring about acceptance. Still, I stand by the premise that the incorrect use of a conjunction creates more problems than it solves. First, a conjunction at the start of a sentence usually creates a sentence fragment. Okay, some sentence fragments add emphasis to writing. Too many fragments, though, and the effect is lost. Repetition sets in. That's the second problem: Once writers feel free to use *and* or *but* to begin one sentence, they often go berserk, intoxicated with the usage.

When I spot one sentence beginning with *but* in a manuscript, I end up spotting dozens, lo, even sometimes hundreds, in the remainder of the manuscript. What happens to the intended impact? It's lost in the drone of repetition.

Because this book does not teach grammar as much as it does methods to improve your creative writing style, you are welcome to break all the rules of grammar and create your own style, but examine the potential consequences. Many fine authors break established grammar rules, but they know to do so only for impact. Otherwise, they stick to the rules. Less-skilled authors who break rules out of defiance or ignorance create dull or out-of-control prose.

And You Can Count on It

Writers may think they need to begin a sentence with a conjunction to create a transition between sentences, as in the following example: *The oil was supposed to last only one day. Yet through a miracle, it lasted eight.* In this case, the easy correction is this: *The oil was supposed to last only one day, yet through a miracle, it lasted eight.*

You will find you don't need every transition. Examine your fragments and delete unnecessary ones. *And you can count on it* becomes *You can count on it. Yet through a miracle it lasted eight* becomes *Through a miracle it lasted eight.* The rewrites lose no impact and break no grammar rules.

Another repair would put the transitional word inside the sentence, such as this rewrite: *Through a miracle, though, it lasted eight.*

As you can see, sentence fragments of the *and* or *but* variety are simple to fix. Quite often all you have to do is delete the superfluous conjunction, and you have a clear, powerful sentence that meets modern standards of English and has all the impact you need. For more clarity, look at the following example: *Jane walked to the edge of the cliff. But she chose not to jump.* With a little bump of the Delete key, you get this: *Jane walked to the edge of the cliff. She chose not to jump.* The simple change reflects better style. Do you think the first form had more impact? Think again. It had even less impact if the rest of a manuscript featured hundreds of other sentences that began with conjunctions.

However and Other Conjunctive Adverbs

Sometimes adverbs serve as conjunctions. Conjunctive adverbs include *also, finally, furthermore, however, indeed, instead, meanwhile, nevertheless, otherwise, still, therefore,* and *thus.* As a whole, the use of conjunctive adverbs will not affect style, but when they appear at the beginning of a sentence, you could be rolling toward trouble.

Of the words in that list, the word *however* pops up most often at the beginning of sentences and becomes a pattern best avoided. When used as an adverb (*However you want your popcorn is fine with me*), the word *however* poses no problems at the beginning of a sentence. When used as a conjunctive adverb, though (*However, if you want butter on your popcorn, you'll have to melt it yourself*), I recommend it be changed. Chances are if an author uses this formation once, it will continue to show up many times at the beginning of sentences in the same manuscript, so beware.

You may be able to tell if you're using *however* as well as other conjunctive adverbs correctly by whether you want to put a comma after the word. If you sense it needs a comma, it doesn't belong as an opening word.

Acceptable: Still searching for his niche, he wanted to pursue a law degree.
Not recommended: Still, he was searching for his niche and wanted to pursue a law degree.
Better: In search of his niche, he still wanted to pursue a law degree.

Acceptable: Also a candidate for mayor, he decided to take the offer of a judgeship.

Not recommended: Also, he was a candidate for mayor, but he decided to take the offer of a judgeship.

Better: Although also a candidate for mayor, he decided to take the offer of a judgeship.

Acceptable: Finally able to talk, the victim identified the perpetrator.

Not recommended: Finally, when the victim was able to talk, she identified the perpetrator.

I won't go into detail about each of the words listed above; you get my drift. What I do want to address individually, though, is the word *meanwhile*. In my opinion, it stands out no matter where it appears. Especially at the beginning of a sentence, though, it reminds me of the old cliché "Meanwhile, back at the ranch." Think twice whenever you use *meanwhile*, and avoid using it as a conjunction at the beginning of a sentence.

Consider the use of *however, also, finally, furthermore, however, indeed, instead, meanwhile, nevertheless, otherwise, still, therefore,* or *thus* at the beginning of a sentence as another opportunity to write better.

Because *however* is one of the most abused conjunctions I see in manuscripts, I'll give you a few more examples to consider.

Weak: However, the weather forecaster had not predicted rain.

Better: The weather forecaster had not predicted rain, however.

Weak: However, John liked Mary more than he did Bertha.

Better: John, however, liked Mary more than he did Bertha.

Weak: However, Golda wanted an engagement ring before she moved to D.C.

Better: Before Golda moved to D.C., though, she wanted an engagement ring.

The rewrites above represent another important part of creative writing: variation. Use the same sentence structure too often, and readers soon feel they can predict what comes next. Predictability creates boredom. In each of the corrected examples, a new sentence structure emerges, and variety is good.

Break a rule once, and you add impact. Break the rule twice, and your writing stalls. Break the rule three or more times, and not only does your writing crash and burn, but you also look like a novice.

So

Although I don't see the conjunction *so* used often at the beginnings of sentences, I do see it. More often it occurs inside a sentence, which is fine at first glance, but because the word *so* has many meanings and functions, writers can overuse it. Consider the use of *so* a warning sign, an opportunity to rewrite and write in style.

Some writers use it in an attempt to show a solution to a posed problem, and a misused use of *so* might look like this:

Writers should avoid repetition. So how do they avoid repetition?

Better: Writers should avoid repetition, but how do they avoid it?

When to Break the Rules

Yes, writers can break rules, and dialogue is the perfect place to break them. In dialogue, we often start our sentences with conjunctions. Remember, though, that we don't use some of the more formal conjunctions in dialogue. When people speak, they more often say "but," rather than "yet" or "however." Remember to keep dialogue informal and conversational, unless your character happens to be extremely proper in manner and speech.

Then There's the Word That Was Not a Conjunction

Then, which can be an adverb or an adjective, is not a conjunction, yet I often see it used incorrectly, as if it were. Example: *Then, we all left for the funeral.* Better: *We all left for the funeral* or *We then all left for the funeral.*

Many times you can delete the word *then*, and it rarely belongs at the beginning of a sentence. The rule of thumb is this: If you can delete a word and the sentence meaning remains the same, delete it. (I could have said *then delete it*, but who needs *then*?)

Conjunctions with Compound Sentences

One of the important rules of creative writing calls for variety in every form. We need variety in our word choices, dialogue styles, sentence structure, and sentence length. If we use all short sentences, the writing grows choppy. If all our sentences tend to be long and compound, the pace drags, and comprehension slows.

We need conjunctions, when used appropriately. Use them in a series (*John, Jake, and Mary saw a wood duck, an ibis, and a heron*). Use them in compound sentences (*John likes hot dogs; however, Mary is a vegetarian*).

To use conjunctions correctly, you also have to understand compound sentences. I see mistakes regarding compound sentences all the time. A compound sentence is one that contains at least two closely related independent clauses. Correct compound sentences, except for short ones, are separated by commas or semicolons. Here are some examples of acceptable correct compound sentences:

The dog ran after the ball, but he did not bring it back.
Lita wrote comic books for a living; however, she really wanted to write mystery novels.
Bryan cooked dinner, and Michael set the table.

It bears repeating that in correct compound sentences, the elements are closely linked. If they are not, break compound sentences into two or more sentences. Example of an incorrect compound sentence: *The dog ran after the ball, and he ate dinner at seven.* The two elements (running after the ball and eating dinner) do not have a close relationship. To correct the issue, break the sentence, perhaps like this: *The dog ran after the ball. He did not return it, because he usually ate dinner at seven. He retrieved his dinner dish instead of the ball.*

Here's another example of a compound sentence, and in this one, until we read further, we won't know the actions are related: *Mary grabbed the phone, but the intruder walked in.* To turn it into a logical compound sentence, the rewrite might go this way: *Mary grabbed the phone, but she never had a chance to dial it before the intruder walked in.*

Compound sentences have a place in any manuscript, but they should not dominate the work. When they appear too often, a pattern emerges, and patterns exhaust readers.

Good writing avoids too many short, choppy sentences as well as too many long sentences. Here's an example of a pleasant combination of short and long sentences:

> Vicki never liked petunias. She planted foxglove, gloxinia, daylilies, red salvia, bachelor buttons, and daisies, but she shied away from anything in the nightshade family. She considered petunias poison.

Ready to Write in Style?

I'll bet you're wondering how your computer can help you be objective about your conjunctions and help you write in style. If you sense you've been loose with your conjunctions, use the Find and Refine Method, but also tell your computer to match the case (which refers to whether the word is capitalized or not—uppercase or lowercase), and type in the word *And* with a capital *A*. Let the computer stop on every use of *And*, so you can eliminate it with revision. You can do the same with other abused words, such as *But, However, So, Or,* and *Then.* Capitalizing the word in the Find function and telling it to match the case allows you to spot every misuse at the start of a sentence, but remember that sometimes, depending on how it is used, *however* can be correct at the beginning of a sentence. Oh, dear! You will have to use your brain after all.

After searching for the words above, type in the following words one at a time, without being case-sensitive (in other words, do not tell the computer to match the case): *and, but, so also, finally, furthermore, indeed, instead, meanwhile, nevertheless, otherwise, still, therefore, then,* and *thus.* Examine the word location. Is it at the beginning of the sentence? Whoops! If it is used as a conjunction, fix it. If it's in the body of the sentence where it belongs, decide whether it represents a series or a compound sentence. If it is a compound sentence, make sure the elements are closely related. Check to see if any other compound sentences appear within two or three sentences of it. When you find too many compound sentences close together, change a few. Break them into separate sentences. Rewrite until you see variation in the whole section you want to improve.

Exercises to Build Your Writing Muscles

Practice using your computer to help you with your writing style. Type in the sentences below and use the Find and Refine Method (match the case) on *And, But, However, So, Or, Yet,* and *Then.* If you think you must link ideas with a conjunction, rewrite the sentences so the conjunction is not at the beginning of the sentence. Next use the Find and Refine Method without matching the case and examine the use of *and, but, so, also, finally, furthermore, indeed, instead, meanwhile, nevertheless, otherwise, still, therefore, then,* and *thus.* Decide whether you need to use these conjunctions at all. If you think you must, be positive that your compound sentences have closely related elements. Whenever you can, consider rewriting into more than one sentence, to avoid overusing any particular conjunction.

As you rewrite the sentences, use your head. Be creative, be visual, and be concise.

1. However small her feet, Bess always thought they looked huge, and she liked to buy purses that matched her outfits.
2. Ann liked to write and even submitted many stories to publishers. But she never sold any of her manuscripts.
3. Dog training takes discipline. So many owners give up and let their dogs run wild and do whatever they want. And untrained dogs annoy people and endanger other animals.
4. The teacher assigned too much homework. Furthermore, he was a strict disciplinarian.
5. Do you want pizza for dinner? Or would a big salad be better?
6. Finally, the package arrived with the scarf I ordered. And it came in the wrong color.
7. She turned to the bellboy and smiled. Then she nodded and slid her key into the lock.
8. Doris spoke about child safety at the conference. Nevertheless, no one remembered her topic.
9. All the cards in this deck are marked. Therefore, we are opening a new deck and we will soon serve hors d'oeuvres.
10. Exercise and diet compound to create a healthy lifestyle. So you must create a schedule that includes exercise. Furthermore, you will improve your thinking processes when you eat right.

Possible rewrites:
1. However small her feet, Bess always thought they looked huge. She often tried to distract people

from her feet, and to do so, she liked to buy purses that matched her outfits.

2. Ann liked to write. She submitted many stories to publishers, but she never sold any of her manuscripts.

3. Dog training takes discipline, so many owners give up and let their dogs run wild. Untrained dogs annoy people and endanger other animals.

4. The teacher assigned too much homework; furthermore, he was a strict disciplinarian.

5. Do you want pizza for dinner, or would a big salad be better?

6. The package finally arrived with the scarf I ordered, but it came in the wrong color.

7. She turned to the bellboy and smiled. She nodded and slid her key into the lock.

8. Doris spoke about child safety at the conference, but no one remembered her topic.

9. All the cards in this deck are marked; therefore, we will open a new deck. Soon we will serve hors d'oeuvres.

10. Exercise and diet compound to create a healthy lifestyle, so you must create a schedule that includes exercise. You will also improve your thinking processes when you eat right.

Whoops! Watch for Manu-slips!

Here are some playful looks at outtakes from unpublished manuscripts. Not all demonstrate incorrectly used conjunctions, but they all deserve a second look, to be sure you don't make the same slips.

- [Opening lines] Scattered clouds high above the Lake captured and refracted the bright morning sunshine with glistening magnificence. Appearing like meticulously jeweled prisms of vapor, the incessant procession drifted lazily across the sky with a peculiar far off silence, an expectant hush charged and galvanized with eventfulness. Frozen into an infinity of obscure and intangible configurations, the pertinacious host of vast billowing white vapor towered enormously against a resplendent blue back-drop. [Need I remark about the abused adjectives?]
- Images of long-barreled rifles and Bowie knives shot through his mind. [Ouch!]
- The plainness of attire together with her black hair accented by contrast the vividness of her face. Steady directness of perceptive gray eyes and a composure of quiet readiness projected a self-assured certainty about herself and her place. [That overwritten sentence contrasted the vividness of my attention span.]
- In turn, each slipper had been tied to the Owner's feet via a tangled web of fishing line, and with each and every step, the lines jumped out to wriggle menacingly like a school of rubber guard eels; hopefully instilling a measure of awe and respect into his intended victims.
- It was the best sort of summer night, when you're not sure whether you're warm or you're cool, and it's all stars and wisps of sounds of people walking out, far enough away you don't have to worry about seeing them but close enough you can hear them now and then, ad if you want you can start wondering about who they are and what their lives are like, which is always a pleasure.

9

TO INFINITIVES AND BEYOND

Once you understand infinitives thoroughly, you will see they often signify an opportunity for more authoritative forms. Infinitives are the basic verb forms preceded by the word *to*, such as *to live, to smile, to jump, to laugh, to talk,* and *to lift.*

An infinitive, the basic building block of English, is comparable to a key. By itself, it can't go anywhere, but it has the potential to drive a sentence once it gets turned the right way. You must transform it from promise to powerful by turning the infinitive into an active form of the verb.

Like engines without petrol, infinitives look fine but go nowhere. Infinitives stall sentences. Infinitives show up in our sentences, but the more infinitives you change into action forms of the verb, the more power you'll give your sentences and the more you'll strengthen your writing. Infinitives give the promise of action, but on their own, they cannot deliver any movement. Spot infinitives by looking for the telltale preposition *to*, which precedes most infinitives, as in *to write.* From the infinitive all other forms of the verb flow, such as these: *I write, you wrote, he writes,* and so forth.

The word *infinitive* comes from the Latin, *infinitus*, which means "infinite" or "not bounded," because infinitives have no reference to a particular tense, person, or subject. Verbs start out as infinitives, their basic form, and because they are merely the beginning, they require manipulation. Turn the key—use the action form of a verb—and you drive the sentence forward. Infinitives beg for stronger, more compelling forms. Later you can open your toolbox—your computer—and use the Find and Refine Method to locate each instance of *to*. For now, let's get into infinitives and beyond.

More About Infinitives

Instead of using infinitives such as *to walk, to dance, to laugh,* let infinitives signal an opportunity for improvement in your writing. Strong writing uses the brawny, active forms of verbs (*I walk, she dances, we laughed*). Writers cannot avoid infinitives, but examine each one. Replace as many as possible with stronger forms, and the writing grows more powerful.

Look at the following, an acceptable sentence: *She started to walk down the hallway, and her shoes began to make squeaking sounds on the linoleum.* The sentence has no grammatical flaws; the punctuation is correct; it's not too long; and the subjects are related enough to warrant the compound sentence.

You probably already write acceptable English, though. Now you want to write potent prose, active English. Turn on the key to your engine, and the result might be this: *She walked down the hallway, and her shoes squeaked on the linoleum.* That change didn't take long, did it?

What makes the second version stronger than the initial one? Several things. The first version boasts eighteen words, the edited version, twelve. Instead of *started to walk,* we cut it down to the action verb, *walked.* We polished *began to squeak* and reached the action verb, *squeaked.* Tighten, tighten, tighten.

Shorter is often better, but not always. Sharp minds observe even more reasons for choosing the second version over the first. In the first version, *to walk* and *to squeak* give no visual image, no action, and no sense of true sound. *Walked* and *squeaked* do.

Save *began* and *started* plus an infinitive for the rare times when action does begin in actuality, such as in the following: *She began to walk when she was two years old.* Another instance of acceptable use might go like this: *She began to walk, but someone stepped off the elevator and bumped into her.*

Whenever possible, turn infinitives, those unstarted engines, into powerful, active, visual verbs.

Don't Plan to Fail

In business writing, one of the most fateful things you can do is write something like this: *We plan to do everything possible to keep our clients happy.*

Nothing is wrong with the construction, but let's examine what would make the sentence better. First, and most obvious, we have two infinitives in the same sentence, *to do* and *to keep*. Avoid repetition. If you take out only one infinitive, which should it be? The decision will be easy, when I tell you the second flaw: *Plan to* is wimpy. Take it out, and the sentence stops being insipid and becomes souped-up: *We do everything possible to keep our clients happy.*

Do I have to delete every infinitive?

No, you don't have to remove every infinitive. They are impossible to avoid altogether. For example, what if I wrote *No, you need not remove every infinitive.* One form of that sentence is no stronger than the other, but the second version is a little stilted. Why use the second form? If a particular paragraph, page, or manuscript has too many instances of *to*, *too*, or *two*, choose the second version, and you reduce the repetition. Repetition jumps off the page at readers. Anything that jars people makes them realize they are reading.

By the way, not every *to* points to an infinitive. *To*, an acceptable preposition or adverb, also indicates the direction, destination, or position of somebody or something. *John led his sister to the water fountain. She pulled up to the curb. Look to your right for the Parliament House.*

For practice, look at the examples below. How would you rewrite them and make them stronger? Type them into your computer and use the Find and Refine Method to find *to* and then rewrite the sentences in style.

After you complete these exercises, use the Find and Refine Method to search some of your own work and replace unnecessary infinitives with stronger forms of the verb. Recast sentences completely, if necessary, and always choose illustrative words, action words. Descriptions—visual and tangible—count in this exercise, which means shorter is not always better.

Apply all the principles you've learned so far, and make each sentence as powerful as you can. Remember that not every *to* signals an infinitive, and you may not be able to eliminate all infinitives (See?).

One last hint: You can keep your computer program from stopping on words that include *to*, such as *together*, *into*, and *total*. When you choose Find, hit your space bar, type *to*, and hit the spacebar again, and your computer will be more selective in its search.

1. Mary wanted to learn to dance, but she was too scared to try.
2. John went to the trouble to find a dictionary.
3. Philip began to pant as he continued to climb the hill.
4. Every time I go to school, the boys start to tease me about my hair.
5. I was about to die of thirst.
6. Whatever happened to the boys who used to play guitar by the fountain?
7. She proceeded to call Tom, but his line was busy.
8. Ellen went to my house to mow the lawn for me.
9. I do not want you to pay for my dinner.
10. Joan's health would not have been the same, without Jim to take care of her.

Your rewrites may differ from the suggestions below, because the answers are neither right nor wrong. Your responses may be even better than the following possible rewrites:

1. Mary's eyes misted when she watched others dance, but fear kept her from trying it herself.
2. John searched until he found a dictionary.
3. Philip panted as he struggled up the hill.
4. The boys at school tease me about my hair.
5. My mouth felt like a dry sponge. I feared I might die, if I did not find water soon.
6. Remember the boys who played guitar by the fountain? I wonder whatever became of them.
7. She dialed Tom's number, but she heard a busy signal.
8. Ellen mowed the lawn for me.

9. Don't pay for my dinner.
10. If Jim had not taken care of Joan, her health would not have been the same.

Whoops! Watch those Manu-slips!

Here are some playful looks at outtakes from unpublished manuscripts. Some may make you giggle, but all have embedded lessons. We can't see our own errors when we make them. I have written the sentences as they appeared, complete with any incorrect syntax, punctuation, or spelling. Only the character names have been changed to protect the property of the authors.

- Marsha walked behind a truck to pick up an ear of corn and waited for it to go forward. [Placement in the sentence means she waited for the ear of corn to go forward.]
- John recognized the aloofness, but was unwilling to breach the subject, either. [He should have broached the subject.]
- As anxious as Marsha was to see John, it prayed on her mind, because of her promise. [This sentence has several errors. It should be as follows: *As eager as Marsha was to see John, it preyed on her mind, because of her promise.*]
- With a discussed look on his face, he preceded to tell me that . . . [I'm sure his look was not the subject of conversation—discussed—and that his dialogue did not come before he could speak. It should have been this way: *With a disgusted look, he told me that . . .*]

- Marsha's eyes grew large and turned to John. [I can imagine a cartoon character whose eyes bug out and turn on their own, but I hope Marsha turned her head, so that she could see John.]
- A few drinks listening to a man with a silver platted voice who seems to be singing just for you can be hard to resist. [I wish I knew a voice that had a silver map, but the correct word choice would have been *plated*. The whole sentence is too awkward to resist.]
- After explaining to the disembodied voice who they were and what they wanted and receiving instructions to see that the reporters were shown off the property the huge iron gates began to swing open. [Oh, how those gates explained before they swung open!]

10

IS YOUR PUNCTUATION LOSING POWER?

Do you know how to use ellipses (. . .) correctly? Do you know when to use em dashes (—)? Are you familiar with en dashes (–) and when to use them? Do you know the correct way to type each punctuation mark? Do you use parentheses ( ) correctly? Can you recognize an exclamation? How many spaces should you type after a period? Punctuation trips up many an excellent writer.

Even if you think you know how to use ellipses, dashes, and other punctuation correctly, you could be wrong. You could also be overusing one or all of these punctuation marks, a flaw I see in many of the manuscripts I edit.

Why should ellipses, dashes, and parentheses—mere punctuation marks—be included in a book on how to improve writing style? Simple. In the manuscripts I edit, ellipses, parentheses, and dashes often incorrectly or inadequately substitute for traditional punctuation and signal an opportunity to strengthen the writing.

For clarification, let me explain that the term *ellipsis* refers to one group of dots, whereas *ellipses* is the plural for more than one group.

Ellipses and dashes have a place in fiction and nonfiction, but parentheses rarely belong in fiction. Learn how to use punctuation marks according to the type of writing you do. Examine them to see if you used them correctly and whether you can replace them with something stronger.

I base much of my information on *The Chicago Manual of Style*, the guidebook most book publishers use. Rather than make you trudge through more than 1,000 pages in *The Chicago Manual of Style*, though, I'll simplify some of its points regarding punctuation. Follow Chicago style, and you increase the chances of your book manuscript getting accepted by a publisher. Self-publishers who follow Chicago style turn out more professional-looking books, too, so all writers need to know the information in this chapter. Potential publication is enough to persuade many writers to follow the guidelines, but for those who want an explanation or are writing something other than fiction, read on.

Ellipses Typography

Chicago style allows two types of typography for ellipses:

1. Three periods with spaces between and a space before and after: *Mrs. Circe . . . Mrs. Circe, can you hear me?* or
2. Three periods with no spaces and no spacing before and after: *Mrs. Circe...Mrs. Circe, can you hear me?*

While either typography method is acceptable, the author must be consistent throughout the manuscript, using only one typestyle or the other for all ellipses.

How Should You . . . Um, Handle Hesitant Dialogue?

Authors and editors often disagree on how to indicate interrupted or faltering dialogue, and some use dashes, while others use ellipses. Worse yet, some authors use dashes in one place and ellipses in another place.

Chicago style clarifies and standardizes the issue. It recommends ellipsis points for hesitating speech intended to show bewilderment, lack of self-confidence, or anguish. Here are some examples of ellipses used correctly:

"I put the coins here . . . that is, there . . . I put them there."
"My outfit...what on earth should I wear?"
Mary's mouth turned down. "But Daddy, I . . . I wanted to . . . to go, too."
"Um...um...," Philip said.

Notice in the last example that a comma after the last ellipses separates the speech from the attribution (*Philip said*).

In each of my examples, the ellipsis marks appear in dialogue. I often see ellipses in narrative, though, which is not recommended, unless perhaps the book is written in first person (*I*). In first person, the narrator is speaking in his or her own voice, so hesitation may sometimes haves a place in such narrative. Having said that, even though bestsellers have been written in first person, I don't recommend writing in first person, because it inherently tells more than it shows and is limiting in many other ways.

Although interrupted and faltering dialogue can differ from manuscript to manuscript, I insist that the author be consistent. Decide how you want to handle certain things in your manuscript and be unwavering throughout. If you are writing a book, follow Chicago style, and you can't go wrong.

Some writers use more than three periods to indicate a long hesitation, but such usage is simply incorrect. Now that you are a more knowledgeable writer, I know you won't make that mistake.

Quotations From Other Sources

Nonfiction, more often than fiction, extracts passages from other sources, and those cases call for ellipses. *The president reported, "Science is the foundation of our university. . . . We need to promote our science department more to the public."* Notice that when the omission encompasses more than a sentence, the ellipsis should have four dots. The first dot is then the period, and it has no space between it and the preceding word. Here is another example:

> *"All meaningful and lasting change starts first in your imagi-*
> *nation. . . . Imagination is more important than knowledge."*
> —Albert Einstein

Dash on Down

The em dash (or the equivalent, two hyphens in a row), according to Chicago style, suggests an intrusion or a change in thought. No space goes before or after an em dash. Here are some em dashes used correctly:

> "I want to—is it okay if I—bring my cat?" (See the change in thought, when the character first wants to state a demand, but instead changes it to a request?)
> Tall weeds and wildflowers grew where the lawn had once been—time had passed.
> Happiness--some say it is a journey, not a destination.

Interruption

Use an em dash or two hyphens to indicate interruption, too.

"What the—"

"Mary, please get--"

When To Use En?

The en dash, which is longer than a hyphen and shorter than an em dash, can be achieved on a computer several ways. The most reliable way is to go to Symbols, select Special Characters, and then select En Dash.

The en dash stands for the word *to*. Writers of fiction almost never need to use en dashes, because fiction rarely calls for symbols to replace words. Writers of nonfiction, however, may want to list an expanse of dates, for example, or a range of numbers.

Read pages 42–64 to learn more about roses.

The officer asked the driver to recite the alphabet backwards, from z–a.

Parentheses (singular: parenthesis)

Although parentheses appear in business English and other nonfiction works (parentheses are the little marks that surround this notation), fiction writers should avoid them. Parentheses snap readers out of the story. Parentheses usually represent author intrusion, too. Place parenthetical information into the sentences, instead, or embed the information elsewhere, so it flows naturally. Here are some examples, with the poor usage first and the same sentences written in style.

Not recommended: Sam (Jean's son) worked in the theater.
Better: Sam, Jean's son, worked in the theater.

Not recommended: "Why is she wearing a babushka (head scarf)?
Better: "Why is she wearing a babushka? Didn't head scarves go out with the hippies?"

When I add information or write an aside, my first inclination is to put it in parenthesis, so I am guilty of overusing parentheses in my rough drafts. In my personal letters, I'm the worst. I see things like the following in my writing: *I went to the store today to buy a raincoat. (I could have gone yesterday, but it was raining, and I didn't have a raincoat to wear to the store!)* In personal letters or e-mail messages, such informal chatter and punctuation would not matter. When I write to sell my work, though, I look it over and find ways to avoid parentheses. If the above example appeared in something I wanted to sell, I would rewrite it, remove the unnecessary parenthesis, and delete the incorrect exclamation mark. The result would be this: *I went to the store today to buy a raincoat. I could have gone yesterday, but it was raining, and I didn't have a raincoat to wear to the store.* The revision maintains the playfulness yet gets the point across without invasive, unnecessary punctuation.

You'll find parentheses scattered in this book, but because it is nonfiction, I can get away with using a few.

Overuse
I see dashes and parentheses overused more often than ellipses, so let's talk about those darned dashes again for a

moment. If you examine each one, you'll find that many replace some other form of punctuation.

Example: John—the tailor—was not impressed.
Better: John the tailor was not impressed or: John, the tailor, was not impressed.

Example: "Sissy--come with me."
Better: "Sissy, come with me."

Example: "I thought of a better way to handle the situation—I threw my hands up in the air and cried for help."
Better: "I thought of a better way to handle the situation. I threw my hands up in the air and cried for help."

I'm harping on the dash, ellipsis, and parenthesis for a reason. The human eye doesn't notice commas and other ordinary punctuation, but dashes, ellipses, parentheses, and colons stand out. For that reason, use them correctly and as sparingly as you would an exclamation mark, which also draws attention to itself.

Hey! What About Exclamation Marks?
Exclamation points or marks (!) should show up only in exclamatory sentences. What the heck is an exclamatory sentence? They often begin with *how* or *what*, without being questions, as in *How awful! What a mess!* An exclamation can be a command, as in *Run for your life! Grab that rope!* It can also be a short burst, such as *Ouch! Rats! Damn!*

Inexperienced writers may find exclamation marks tempting. In a failed attempt to put emphasis on a sentence or show surprise, they end many comments with exclamation marks. Don't be reeled in by this mistake! Editors call the technique "schoolgirl style," and if you want to succeed in your writing efforts, you will not write in schoolgirl style.

Here are some examples of incorrect usage of punctuation marks: *"I really love your dress!" She threw down the bucket! He dropped to his knees and proposed! She looked up and saw a bear!*

When I see one exclamation mark in a manuscript, I see dozens, or even hundreds, and most will be incorrect. If you see exclamations in your manuscripts, think twice. They are trying to tell you something.

Instead of exclamation marks, rely on good writing to show surprise or other emotions. Let's review the above examples and see what good writing might do to avoid the exclamation marks: *"I really and truly adore your dress." She slammed the bucket to the ground. He dropped to his knees and, to her shock, proposed. She looked up, and a huge bear loomed over her.* You can probably rewrite the sentences even better. Feel free to do so.

According to the rules of punctuation, exclamation marks have no place in narrative, unless you write in first person. If your words don't convey passion, exclamation marks won't help. William Styron, author of *Sophie's Choice*, said, "Every writer should be given just one exclamation mark per career." Follow his advice, and you too might write a book that sells more than two million copies and becomes a major motion picture.

Slash/Burn Virgules

What's a virgule? It's the proper term for a slash, most often used in either/or situations (see?) such as this one: *John Hartford was a singer/dancer/songwriter.*

Stylish writing avoids virgules. A stronger way to write the sentence would be this: *John Hartford wrote songs, performed them, and danced.*

Virgules have a place in business writing at times, but in fiction and nonfiction, one of the worst offenses you can make is to have a character speak with slashes. Here's an example of poor dialogue using virgules: *"I must dust/mop/vacuum before I leave the house."* Instead, *"I must dust, mop, and vacuum before I leave the house"* works better.

You may use a virgule on the rare occasion when a character is a businessperson accustomed to speaking in jargon, but write the dialogue the way the character spoke it. It might come out this way: *"Richard, your job will be public relations slash receptionist, until we hire another employee."*

Bracket This

Like virgules and parentheses, brackets have no place in fiction. If you use them, *The Chicago Manual of Style* dictates that brackets go inside parentheses. *Jeremy held only two jobs in his life (one when he was a teen [newspaper delivery] and one when he graduated from medical school [doctor]).*

In nonfiction, brackets delineate author notes when parenthetical information is included inside other information, as in this example: *Michener, American writer of historical novels, produced many books, including* Tales of the South Pacific *[ed. note: He won a Pulitzer Prize for that one], and* The Source.

As an aside, you might note in the above example that when something such as a book title, which should be italicized, appears within a sentence written in italics, the words that would have been italicized should then be in roman type, not italicized.

Periods

Yes, I'm sure you know to use periods at the end of sentences, but controversy still arises among writers as to whether to space once or twice after a period. Let me put that question to rest.

Many of us learned to type on typewriters, and when we did, our teachers instructed us to hit the spacebar twice after every period and colon. Such spacing had a reason, back in the days of typewriters, but that reason is gone with the advent of computers. When we type on computers, we must space only once after periods. The logic of that change has to do with layout, once a manuscript is set in justified type, but I won't go into details. Just know this: break the two-space habit. Hit the spacebar only one time after each period or colon.

Especially if you plan to self-publish, you absolutely must not have extra spaces in a manuscript that goes to press, or the extra spacing will make the printed book look awkward.

If you simply can't break the two-space habit, I have a simple solution for repairing all those incorrect spaces. It's a good idea to use the same method to catch any extra spacing that has crept into a manuscript, because extra spaces can creep in whenever we make a change to the copy.

Use my Find and Refine Method™ to find and delete all the extra spaces, and the task takes only a few seconds for an entire manuscript, no matter how long it may be. In my current version of Word, I use Control+H to bring up the Find and Replace window. I put the cursor in the dialogue box for Find and press the space bar twice. In the Replace box, I put the cursor in the box and press the spacebar once. I push the button that says Replace All, and in moments, the computer makes all the changes for me.

When I work with clients' manuscripts, I sometimes have to run the function more than once to ensure I catch all the extra spaces. Run it until the computer says it has made zero replacements, and the job is finished.

More Computer Help

Type in all the sentences below. One at a time, use the Find and Refine Method—that is, use the Find function on your computer—to locate and examine every dash, ellipsis, parenthesis, exclamation mark, virgule, and bracket. Delete as many as possible, rewrite, and write in style.

1. The workshop defined fiction . . . not that we did not know the meaning of the word.
2. The invitation to the party—the one planned for late December—included a request for donations to a political organization.
3. Even though he considered himself a singer/songwriter, Rick found work in Nashville as a janitor/security guard.
4. A good pair of binoculars (preferably those with autofocus) help bird watchers catch elusive species in the fields and along riverbanks.
5. Thomas did a great job! He garnered pledges of over $3,000 to our fund-raiser (the one for Special Olympics).
6. Wait! I have a memo I want you to read—if you have the time.
7. "I never . . . that is, I don't think I ever ate sweetbreads before, but if you want me to (and you obviously do), then I will at least taste them."

8. Please do not fax or e-mail manuscripts (send them only by regular mail) and always follow guidelines (available on our website).

9. The moon shone orange/yellow as it rose above the horizon.

10. Handle all irate customers with care . . . do not cause a scene—acknowledge their discontent and ask what would make the situation better for them.

Possible rewrites. Remember that not every example is wrong as written.

1. The workshop defined fiction, not that we did not know the meaning of the word.

2. The invitation to the party planned for late December included a request for donations to a political organization.

3. Even though he considered himself a singer/songwriter, Rick found work in Nashville as a janitor/security guard. Note: I like this particular sentence, even with the virgules, because of the implied humor in it. A rewrite might ruin the humor. Remember that creative writing sometimes does break the "rules."

4. A good pair of binoculars, preferably ones with autofocus, help bird-watchers catch elusive species in the fields and along riverbanks.

5. Thomas did a great job. He garnered pledges of more than $3,000 to our Special Olympics fundraiser.

6. Wait! I have a memo I want you to read, if you have the time.

7. "I never . . . that is, I don't think I ever ate sweetbreads before, but if you want me to, and you obviously do, then I will at least taste them."

8. Please do not fax or e-mail manuscripts. Send them by regular mail only, and always follow the guidelines available on our website.

9. The moon shone a yellow-orange as it rose above the horizon.

10. Handle all irate customers with care. Do not cause a scene. Acknowledge the customer's discontent and ask what would make the situation better.

Pardon Me; Your Manu-slip Is Showing

Once again I'll feature excerpts from unedited manuscripts, with all typos and other errors intact the way I received them.

- I have written 20 books all Fiction. They include childrens, poems, adult, and Erotic all unpublished! I also do the art work and write music. I wrote all 20 books on my SS check. Can you help me get a contract before my mother goes to heaven. I would like her to rest in peace now. [I'd like to see the check with the books on it.]

- Like a flare in the nighttime sky, Ed's sparkler lit up the darkness as the juices popped, crackled, and fizzled into the light—the light shining inside Ed's illuminated brain. [I've heard of flashes of brilliance, but this example isn't one of them.]

- I selected your agency as one with interest and expertise in novels of the thriller/espionage/action genre to whom I am writing after referring to the "Guide to Literary

Agents." [The writer needs to know to whom he or she is writing novels.]

- His quietly reserved distinguished features with attentive blue-gray eyes, firm set of mouth and chin betrayed nothing of most unusual self-conscious constraint since this trial began the week before. [This sentence betrays nothing of most logic.]

11

OTHER FINDS FOR FINER WRITING

So far, we've been traveling the back roads of creative writing, cruising slowly, going into detail about singular subjects that represent opportunities for improvement. I'm about to accelerate into more than a dozen small ways you can improve what you write and write in style.

I may surprise you with a few subjects, because you see them in print, but never knew you could do better, with a few tips from a book doctor.

Fasten your seat belt; here we go.

Presently

Guess what. *Presently* does not, in its preferred usage, mean *at present*. It means *in a little while*. Yup, the following statement is wrong: *The school is presently looking for funding*. It should be either *The school is currently looking for funding* or even better, *The school is looking for funding*. Why is the second version better? Because, as is often the case, the adverb *currently* is redundant, as used.

Notice how you can delete *currently* or *presently* without losing anything? Remember what I said about deleting anything you don't need? Get it? Good.

Here is an example of *presently* used correctly: *The men waited in their cells, and presently their attorney arrived.*

Presently has been misused so often that some circles have accepted it to mean *currently*. You, however, want your prose to sparkle in all circles, so you won't muddy your expressions, right? When you use tarnished prose because others do it, you're a driver who thinks no one cares how the car looks, as long as it gets you to your destination. If your destination is a junk pile, the looks of the car won't matter, but if you want to sell your car—the same as you want to sell your manuscript, proposal, or product—you'll be sure to take out a chamois and bring out the shine.

Whenever tempted to use the word *presently*, think twice. Do you mean *currently*? If so, write *currently*. Better yet, delete it, and the meaning remains the same.

Unacceptable: The policy presently requires prepayment.
Acceptable: The policy currently requires prepayment.
Better: The policy requires prepayment.

Again, use *presently* to mean in a short time from the present. *The school will look for funding presently. I'll join you presently.*

A few of my more astute readers will want to hit the brakes and say, "Hold it right there, Bobbie. You said to avoid adverbs." You're right. Now you have two reasons to stop a moment and rethink your word choice when tempted to use *presently*. If you can delete it without changing the meaning of your sentence, do so.

Use the Find and Refine Method to find *presently* and repair or delete misuses.

As I Was Saying

The word *as* is commonly overused in the manuscripts I edit. It appears to be a harmless little word, and many writers can't find any other way to show action unfolding without using it. Example: *He spoke in sharp tones as he drove the car.*

All by itself, the word *as* does no harm. Where it does damage is in its overuse. Relate repetition to engine noises. If you hear your engine make an odd noise one time, you might notice it, but it won't bother you, because it happened only once and went away quickly. If your engine makes the same noise every time you start your car, drive up a hill, or turn a corner, though, you will anticipate the noise, dread it, and wish it would go away. Before long, you'll take your car in for a tune-up or repairs to get relief from that darned racket. Repetition of any sound in prose, too, should result in a tune-up.

Why does *as* get overused so easily? I'm glad you asked. Bear with me, because the upcoming list may bore you, but I have a reason for being blatant.

The word *as* has many uses, including the following:

Equally: *The dog smelled as rank as a moldy towel.*
For instance: *The veterinarian took care of farm animals, as in cows, sheep, and pigs.*
When considered in a specified relation: *The author's second book was good, as opposed to the first one.*
To the same degree: *The incident was not as bad as the reporters described it, but it was so bad as to get media attention.*
In the same way, like: *Actors act as their characters would.*
While: *I raked my fingers through my hair as I ran out to greet him.*

Because: *I listened to President Obama's speech, as I cared about the issues.*

With the result that: *He was so foolish as to lie.*

Though: *Skilled as the speaker was, he could not hold the attention of the audience.*

In accordance with which: *The museum exhibit inspired me, as I expected.*

That, which, who: *Deb ordered the same meal as Al did.*

In the role of: *Cecil stepped in as the teacher.*

In a manner similar to: *The students protested as one.*

Despite: *Fit as he appears, he has a heart condition.*

Time when: *As a young boy, he put rocks in his mouth to stop himself from stuttering.*

Introducing a clause: *As I recall, Ruth ate a salad that night.*

What: *She does as she wants.*

What a long list of definitions! Are you as overwhelmed as I am?

If an author uses the word *as* only once per page, even with a new definition each time, the word still becomes repetitive. Many of my clients use it more than once a page, and most often to mean *at the same time as*. *Nancy took a deep breath as she entered the room*. When I edit printed manuscripts, I often circle and link many of the uses of *as*, to show my clients when they overuse the word. Most clients these days prefer for me to edit their electronic files, though, rather than printed manuscripts, which means I have to tell them to use the Fine and Refine Method to seek and destroy the overuse of the word *as* in their own manuscripts.

Don't be afraid to use *while, when, like, because, though,* and all the alternate words available to writers. To use the Find and Refine Method to help you avoid overusing *as*, in the Find window first hit the spacebar once, type *as* followed by another space, to make your computer find the word you are seeking. If you don't type the spaces, it will stop on the *as* part of words such as *assume, lassitude, assure, pastime, assault, sassy, has, reassign, fantastic,* and so forth. Once your computer finds *as* in your manuscript, see how often the same word appears on the page. If possible, limit your usage to one every three or four pages. If you can use *as* only once a chapter, you're a champion.

Like I Said

Many teachers and editors say you should never fear using the word *said* when writing dialogue. I agree, to a degree. Authors should not go to odd lengths to avoid using *said* in dialogue attributions, sometimes called tags. In a sentence such as the following, *Susan said* is the attribution, or tag: *"I'm going to wait for the bus," Susan said.* The sentence has no flaws, but we're not looking for mistakes only; we're looking for ways to write in style.

One way to write in style is to stay visual, whenever possible; show, rather than tell. *Said* has little action to it, and it has no visual aspects. Some writers avoid *said* and dredge up a long list of other attributions, such as *added, answered, asserted, commented, begged, cried, declared, decried, expressed, hissed, growled, grumbled, mumbled, explained, recalled, replied, repeated, retorted, returned, responded, remarked,* or hundreds of similar words.

If you must attribute a quotation, don't be afraid of the standard *said* or *asked,* because readers find standard words less intrusive than the countless overblown replacements such as *groused, interpreted, interjected, effused, contended, surmised, emphasized,* and such. Yes, I've seen them all and then some.

All these words, the odd and the ordinary attributions, represent an opportunity to write in style. Do so by replacing the attributions with action. Action allows readers to see characters doing things, and we visualize the scene.

When you use action, the writing shows, rather than tells.

> **Attribution through tag:** John commented, "I just came from the dental hygienist. Can you tell?"
>
> **Attribution through action:** John ran his tongue over his teeth. "I just came from the dental hygienist. Can you tell?"
>
> **Attribution through tag:** Marsha remarked, "I have something to tell you about the car."
>
> **Attribution through action**: Marsha cleared her throat. "I have something to tell you about the car."

The "ing" Connection

Perhaps you think your attribution has action, but if it includes an "ing" word, think again. Example: *"Have some turkey," Mrs. Canestraro said, pointing to the platter.*

Improve the action and make it stronger by deleting the "ing" phrase. Use only the action, as in this revision: *"Have some turkey." Mrs. Canestraro pointed to the platter.*

The "ing" connection adds words and sets up repetition often continued throughout a manuscript.

> **Attribution plus "ing" action:** "Yes," Hal said, pushing back his chair.
>
> **Better—attribution through action alone:** "Yes." Hal pushed back his chair.

The same room for improvement applies to attribution that includes the word *as*:

> **Attribution plus action:** "The eggplant is superb," Ed said as he dabbed his lips with the corner of a napkin.
> **Attribution through action alone:** "The eggplant is superb." Ed dabbed his lips with the corner of a napkin.

Inverted Attributions

Inverted attributions, where the attribution precedes the noun or pronoun showing who spoke, may be an attempt to avoid sounding ordinary, but inverted attributions can get out of hand. Here's a normal attribution: *"I'll go first," Ezekiel said.* Here's the inverted form: *"I'll go first," said Ezekiel.* An occasional inversion of the attribution does not draw much attention, but some writers go overboard with them, and they therefore grow repetitive.

If you must use *said*, at least don't make it stick out like a branch caught on your bumper. With too much use, inverted attributions drag down the writing. They appear stilted, grow repetitive, and indicate careless writing.

Inversion disappears when action replaces the attribution or tag. Either of the following examples works fine, and the choice depends upon the order in which the author would like to show the scene unfold: *"Show me to the stove." Sanford settled a chef's toque on his head.* Or: *Sanford settled a chef's toque on his head. "Show me to the stove."*

Toward a More Perfect Manuscript

Which is correct, *toward* or *towards*? Every day of our lives, we hear and see both words. How are we to know when to use each? Should we always use one and never the other?

Let *towards* be a flashing caution light. *The Associated Press Stylebook,* which outlines the style adopted by most periodicals, says always to use *toward* instead of *towards*. *Merriam-Webster* lists the two as synonyms, but lists *towards* as a variant. Strong writers avoid variants. Even *Encarta World English Dictionary,* published in the United Kingdom, where *towards* is used most often, lists *towards* as a variant, and again, I urge writers never to use variants.

You may not be wrong to use *towards,* but after a while, it draws attention to itself, like having one headlight out. Eventually, a broken headlamp will catch the attention of a diligent police officer the way the use of *towards* will offend a knowledgeable client, agent, or publisher. Always use preferred words, rather than variants. Have I pounded the thought well enough into your brain?

One more note about *toward*. Used correctly, it means *in the direction of.* Be careful not to use *toward* when you mean *to*. I see that flaw often in manuscripts. Avoid a sentence like this: *He went toward the door and opened it.* Correct: *He went to the door and opened it.* Also correct: *He started toward the door, but stopped.*

Over/More Than

Strict grammarians do not use *over* when they mean *more than*. I have read that the use of *over* to mean *more than* is becoming acceptable, but "becoming acceptable" does not mean that something has become the standard. I want serious writers everywhere to stick to the rules and avoid things that are only now becoming acceptable. Until a usage becomes standard, I consider it wrong.

Wrong: He's over eighty years old.
Correct: He's more than eighty years old.
Wrong: We have been in business over twenty years.
Correct: We have been in business more than twenty years.

For clarity, always use *over* literally.

Correct: The dog jumped over the barrel.
Correct: Lola wore a coat over her sweater.
Correct: The troops crossed over the bridge

You can sometimes delete *over*, with no change in meaning.

Acceptable: Willy moved over toward Jeannette.
Better: Willy moved toward Jeannette.

Acceptable: On Christmas Day, the family comes over to my house.
Better: On Christmas Day, the family comes to my house.

Amidst, Amongst

I've said it before; don't use variants. *Amidst* and *amongst* are Briticisms and don't belong in American publications. If you write for American publications, use *amid* and *among*.

Incorrect: We have been amidst a big depression.
Correct: We have been amid a big depression.
Incorrect: Janet was amongst those listed as missing.
Correct: Janet was among those listed as missing.

Do you think you never make that mistake? You'd be surprised. I see British terminology like *amidst* and *amongst* in the most otherwise intellectual writings. Perhaps the authors thought that using such words elevated the writing and made the author sound more educated. Not so. Your writing sounds best when you write in style.

Don't Drug Readers

On the opposite end of the spectrum, I often see *drug* used incorrectly as the past tense of *drag*. The past tense of the verb to *drag* is *dragged*.

Maybe writers think using *drug* for past tense sounds current, "with it." Maybe writers don't know any better, because they've heard *drug* used incorrectly so often that they think it is correct. It's a bitter pill to swallow, but *drug* is the present tense of *drug*, not the past tense of *drag*. Here's an example of *drug* used incorrectly: *The killer drug the body across the floor.* Corrected version: *The killer dragged the body across the floor.*

Used correctly, the verb to *drug* means *to give someone a drug* or *to stupefy or dull with a drug*. Do you want to stupefy your readers? I hope not. You'll look like a dope if you use *drug* incorrectly.

Here's an example of *drug* used correctly in present tense: *To ensure my dental patients feel no pain, I drug them before I pull their teeth.* Here's *drug* used correctly in past tense: *The ether drugged the victim into submission.*

Another Sneaky Word

Is anything wrong with the following sentence? *Jane snuck into the kitchen and raided the refrigerator.* Besides the fact that Jane's about to ruin her trim waistline, the writer has lost his or her credibility. The preferred way to write the above sentence is this way: *Jane sneaked into the kitchen and raided the refrigerator.*

Granted, English is a changing language. Some conversational words, even though incorrect, gradually become acceptable in print. When we write dialogue, we use conversational English, to be sure our writers sound realistic. When we write narrative, though, we should avoid variants, slang, nonstandard uses, and misuses. Yes, when we talk, we say *snuck* instead of *sneaked*. We also say things such as *wadn't* instead of *wasn't* and *could of* when we mean *could have*, but we would not write *wadn't* or *could of* in narrative, would we? Of course we wouldn't.

Snuck is not an acceptable form of the past tense of *sneak*. It is a variant, and if you have learned nothing else, you know by now to avoid variants. Use *sneaked*.

Write in Style on a Daily Basis

Always write tight.

Instead of: Jean paid her bills on a weekly basis.
Choose: Jean paid her bills weekly
Or: Jean paid her bills every week.

Instead of: Barry reconciled his bank statements on a monthly basis.
Choose: Barry reconciled his bank statements monthly.

Instead of: Mildred received royalty payments on an annual basis.
Choose: Mildred received royalty payments once a year.

Look Here!

As you are learning, many words work fine in some forms and uses, yet not in others. The word *look* is acceptable as a verb that means "to employ sight." Example: *Golda looked through the window.* I won't give you a hard time for that usage; it's fine.

When used other ways, though, *look* signals an opportunity for improvement. Example: *Golda looked younger than her fifty years.* In that case, *look* has been used as a linking verb, a verb with no action, and we have already discussed why to avoid static verbs. A revision might show, instead: *Golda's unlined face revealed the image of someone younger than her fifty years.*

When you find the word *look* in your work, consider how you have used it. Ponder whether you could write in style with another word choice or a sentence revision. Be careful, though, because some of the alternatives are equally iffy. As an example, let's examine the use of *looking, looked to be* and *looked like.*

I don't recommend any of the following formations:

The young-looking man approached the counter.
He looked to be about twenty.
He looked like he had not eaten in days.

What can you do? Consider these rewrites:

The youthful man approached the counter.
I guessed his age to be twenty.
His skin hung off his bones, as if he had not eaten in days.

Whenever you see any phrase that includes the word *look*, consider writing in style using stronger, more creative words. When you try to stop using *looked*, you may be tempted to use *appeared*, but you haven't moved far enough from the starting line. Remember *appeared* is also a linking (inactive, static) verb, the same as some uses of *look*. Instead of *He looked to be under twenty*, consider this: *His full head of hair and unwrinkled face made Mel guess the man's age to be under twenty*. The first description tells; the second one shows.

Instead of *Bob looked like he had come from the jungle*, consider this: *Bob's T-shirt showed huge sweat stains around the neck and under the arms. He had scratches on his cheek, and blood dripped down one arm*. Which description tells, and which one shows?

Looking for more?

Use caution when tempted to write statements such as these:

Not recommended:

She was dowdy-looking.

A new-looking limousine pulled up to the curb.

He was exhausted-looking.

Looking, when used in the ways above, can be deleted or changed into an active verb, to make a statement stronger. Describe the scene or character. Let your readers decide what constitutes dowdy, new, or worn. In addition, I have already recommended avoiding hyphenated adjectives.

Potential rewrites:

Her colorless dress hung off her thin frame. (dowdy)

A shiny, limousine pulled up to the curb. (new)

His eyes hung half closed, and his shoulders slumped. (exhausted)

Redundancy

In chapter four we discussed how adverbs create redundancies. If the word *pleonasm* means nothing to you, you're in the majority. Even so, every day, you use and hear pleonasms. *Pleonasm* refers to the use of superfluous words. I am sure you have heard or read phrases such as these:

I thought to myself, "Can this be right?"

Come in today, and you'll get a free gift.

She gently tiptoed to the baby's crib.

He gave her a teeny tiny diamond.

She made future plans.

After his wife died, Jerry reverted back to his old habits.

Here are the same sentences without the pleonasms:

I thought, "Can this be right?"

Come in today, and you'll get a gift.

She tiptoed to the crib.

He gave her a tiny diamond.

She made plans.

After his wife died, Jerry reverted to his old habits.

Because many parts of our bodies are specialized, redundancies sometimes occur when people speak of action with our bodies. For example, *He held the rock in his hand*. We cannot hold things with our feet, ears, or hair, so in this case, *in his hand* is redundant. If, however, a character held a rock between his knees or in his teeth, readers would want to know; otherwise we assume when characters hold something, it is with their hands, and saying so would be redundant. *He waved his hand to say good-bye*. We can wave only with our hands, so *his hand* is redundant.

Here are a few more examples of redundancies with our body parts:

> In defiance, she stomped her foot and walked out.
> He flailed his arms in the air.
> She shook her head in disbelief.
> He nodded his head in agreement.
> Elton shrugged his shoulders.

Simplified, your sentences need only be as follows:

> He held the rock.
> He waved good-bye.
> In defiance, she stomped and walked out.
> He flailed.
> She shook her head.
> He nodded.
> Elton shrugged.

Other redundancies I've seen in manuscripts included *baby puppy, cold sleet, wet rain, ask questioningly,* and *nod affirmatively*. Notice how most adverbs are redundant? Good. I'm getting through to you.

The word *pleonasm* comes from the Greek word, *pleonasmos,* "to be in excess." To say more would be redundant.

Life Has Its Ups and Downs

Other sometimes-superfluous words include *up* and *down.* Examples: *Joseph sat down and carved the roast.* Better: *Joseph sat and carved the roast. Etta climbed up the ladder.* Better: *Etta climbed the ladder.*

You cannot delete every instance of *up* and *down,* but whenever you can delete a word without changing the meaning of the sentence, do it, and you write in style.

She Stood Where?

Sam, stunned by the sight of the fire, just stood there and stared.

What's wrong with that sentence? Nothing. What? Did you forget for a second that I'm speaking of improvement, rather than the difference between right and wrong? Gotcha.

Avoid using *sat there* and *stood there,* because *there* is unnecessary. Instead of *Sam, stunned by the sight of the fire, just stood there and stared,* consider *Stunned, Sam stared at the fire.* Instead of *Robert sat there and thought,* use *Robert sat and thought.*

Would You? Could You?

Auxiliary verbs, such as forms of *have, can,* or *will,* accompany main verbs and make distinctions in mood, voice, and tense. In the following example, *have* and *could* are auxiliary verbs: *The carpenters have worked long enough that they could recognize a bad board from fifteen feet away.* While nothing is wrong with the example, overuse of auxiliary verbs results in verbosity.

Many times *would* or *could* are superfluous. One use sets the mood or verb tense, and more uses result in overkill.

I often see *would* and *could* and other auxiliary verbs overused. For example, I see sentences like these:

My mother would sleep until noon every day.
To his right, he could see a flashing red light.

Most of the time, past tense is better, as in these recasts:

My mother slept until noon every day.
To his right, he saw a flashing red light.

Would, an auxiliary verb, is the past tense of *will*. Save it to use in these instances:

1. After a statement of desire, request, or advice*: She wished he would visit.*
2. To make a polite request: *Would you lend me your rake?*
3. To indicate uncertainty: *The book would seem to be improving.*

Avoid using *would* as an auxiliary verb, as in this example: *My teacher would always give me too much homework.* Choose instead: *My teacher always gave me too much homework.*

Could is also an auxiliary verb, the past tense of *can*. Think twice before using *could*, because it often leads to weakened action. For example, instead of *Sandra could see the traffic light ahead* or *Dr. Lee could detect a tumor in the dog's leg*, use the undiluted verb for stronger sentences. *Sandra saw the traffic light ahead* or *Dr. Lee detected a tumor in the dog's leg.*

Real Writing in Style

Strong writers do not use *real* to mean *very*. Like the word *very*, *real* adds nothing, even though we may think it adds emphasis to our words. Let the words be their own emphasis. For instance, instead of *real hot*, use *fiery*. Instead of *real loose*, choose *unrestrained*. Use *real* only to mean *genuine*.

You can delete *real* and *very* almost every time they appear; however, you can use them as an opportunity for improvement. Wherever *real* or *very* appears, find a more creative adjective or verb. Instead of *I was real sorry I opened the box*, consider *I was remorseful that I opened the box*. Even better: *I rued the day I opened the box*.

Instead of *She was real sloppy about her work*, consider *She performed slipshod work*.

Just One More Thing

Like *as*, *just* has many meanings. As an adverb, *just* can mean any of the following:

Precisely: *The train arrived just as we drove up.*
Exactly: *The price came to a dollar, just as I expected.*
Only a moment ago: *I just saw my scar for the first time.*
By a narrow margin: *I just missed the bus.*
Barely: *The dress was cut so low that it just covered her breasts.*
At a little distance: *I reached for the ring, but it was just beyond my reach*
Merely: *I just have a quarter to my name.*
Only: *Just two puppies were in the litter.*
Simply: *I just want to go home.*
Certainly: *Mary just felt thankful she wasn't hurt.*

Perhaps: *Were you thinking you could just leave?*
Possibly: *I just might be there.*
For emphasis: *Just what do you think you're doing?*

Writers most often use *just* when they want to emphasize a point, but if you stop for a moment and think about the sentence, if the wording doesn't emphasize the point enough without *just*, rewrite it. For example, if you feel compelled to write a sentence such as *John just stayed at home all day,* reconsider. Perhaps the point would be stronger if written this way: *Above all else, John preferred to loll around the house all day.* Think about it, and you can come up with an even better rewrite than mine.

Instead of using *just*, choose the explicit adverb you mean or, if possible, delete *just* entirely, because adverbs often are superfluous.

Let's revisit a few of the prior examples of *just* used as an adverb and see what happens to them when we delete it:

The train arrived as we drove up.
The price came to a dollar, as I expected.
I saw my scar for the first time.
I missed the bus.

We didn't do any harm, did we? See how easy it is to rub out an unnecessary word?

Remember, I am speaking of *just* used as an adverb. When you use *just* as an adjective or noun referring to justice, being honorable and fair, fitting, or morally right, you do not have to change or delete it. Examples: *After ten hours of deliberation, the jury reached a just verdict. The actor earned her just deserts.*

Okay, time for a little digression. For those who think the last phrase in that example should be *just desserts*, let me explain. *Desserts*, with two *s*'s in the middle, means a sweet treat after a meal. As used, though, the word *deserts*, with only one *s* in the middle, means *that which one deserves*. *Desert*, an archaic word, is rarely used outside the phrase *just deserts* anymore.

Now back to the subject of the word *just*. To locate misuses of *just*, type "(space) just (space)" into your Find function. Use the Find and Refine Method to see how many times you find *just* in your manuscript. Delete *just* and see if the sentence reads as well as it did before. Many times it will read better. Whenever possible, just delete *just*!

Whip Out Your Rag and Polish Your Prose

If you have a vague feeling that you may have used any of the words discussed in this chapter in a less-than-creative way, use the Find and Refine Method for each item. Examine and repair any details that help you write in style.

I am sad to say that we cannot pick up every redundancy with the Find and Refine Method. We have to use our eyes and brain as we go through the editing process.

Here are some words that a computer can find for you, though, so you can improve the sentences where they appear.

- amidst
- amongst
- as
- basis
- could
- drug

- down
- hand
- head
- just
- look
- looking
- over
- presently
- responded
- said
- snuck
- myself
- real
- there
- towards
- up
- would

An Ounce of Practice

Mahatma Gandhi once said, "An ounce of practice is worth more than tons of preaching." Here, then, is your opportunity for an ounce of practice. Type in all the sentences below. One at a time, use the Find and Refine Method—that is, use the Find function of your software—to locate and examine every word listed above. Delete as many as possible, rewrite, and write in style.

1. On a weekly basis, our teacher would assign homework that had to be completed over the weekend.
2. Sandy is real interested in the show presently on TV.

3. Jean snuck into the basement towards the end of the party.
4. Mike nodded his head just as the girl said, "Want a drink?"
5. Over a year ago, Jane drug herself to the doctor, after she had lain there in bed too long.
6. *I'll never get out alive,* I thought to myself.
7. Has the love amongst us stood up to the test of time?
8. Bedraggled looking, Rick drug himself through the doorway as the band began to play.
9. "Hell hath no fury like a woman shorn," I said as I laughed.
10. Marie just sat there amidst her flowers, thinking to herself that she should at least wave her hand at the visitors.

Possible rewrites:
1. Every week, our teacher assigned homework we had to complete over the weekend. (Remember, *over* is not always wrong!)
2. Sandy is interested in the show on TV.
3. Jean sneaked into the basement toward the end of the party.
4. Mike nodded when the girl said, "Want a drink?"
5. More than a year ago, Jane dragged herself to the doctor, after she had lain in bed too long.
6. *I'll never get out alive,* I thought.
7. Has the love among us stood the test of time?

8. Bedraggled, Rick dragged himself through the doorway when the band began to play. (Better yet, describe how Rick looked.)
9. I laughed. "Hell hath no fury like a woman shorn."
10. Marie sat amid her flowers, thinking she should at least wave at the visitors.

Whoops!

Here are a few more Manu-slips to tickle your funny bone.

- After serving the tea that I'd made earlier that morning and which was cold and delicious with a dash of juice from my own lemons that grew in the back garden, I sat down again. [After reading this sentence, I wanted to collapse too.]
- Long after dark, with a full day of frightened temptation behind me, before dozing off, in a flash of exuberance, I remember the name. [Five introductory phrases are enough to make me forget my own name and wonder what this sentence is about.]
- John progressed on, advancing an inclusive examination. [An agent who reads a sentence like that one is likely to progress on to the next manuscript.]
- John studied his patient's strained features that projected antagonizing pain. [Should be *agonizing* pain, but it's still redundant.]
- John disengaged the hand holding. [Engaged or not, *handholding* should be one word, but readers are already disengaged, so it probably won't matter.]
- Mary relaxed comfortably. [Could she relax any other way?]

- I tore off the covering wrapper. [Did you uncover the redundancy?]
- She examined her written notes.
- "I am a total celibate," he declared. [Can one be a partial celibate?]
- The cans clattered noisily down the stairs.
- John shouted loudly.
- The house was nestled cozily in the valley. [Have you ever seen a house nestled restlessly?]
- I could not get over the gastronomical taste.

12

DON'T KEEP YOUR EYES ON THE ROAD

This tip may insult, astound, or frustrate you with its limitations, but for sure it will amuse you. To make your writing as strong as possible, don't keep your eyes on the road. Keep them in your head. Leave the eyes of your characters in their heads, as well. Eyes can gaze, open wide, close, blink, fog over, mist up, overflow with tears, look around, spot items, and do many wonderful things. Don't, however, let them go wandering around by themselves.

While editing manuscripts, I've read sentences that imply that eyes can dash off, fall out, go for a walk, glue themselves to objects, and perform other tricks.

I've collected close to a hundred "roving eye" excerpts from unedited manuscripts. Some of the sentences almost made me gag. Others brought laughter. Others confused me.

Let's examine the following excerpt: *Experiencing a sudden wave of nausea, Mark's eyes bolted open.* Of course the writer knew what he or she meant. As a reader, we have a good idea of what the writer meant, too. Think about the sentence a moment, though. As written it means Mark's eyes were sick to their stomach, an odd thought, indeed. To further confuse me, how can eyes bolt open? *Bolt,* when used as a verb, means any of the following: to secure or lock as if with a bolt; to arrange or roll (lengths of cloth, for example) on or in a bolt; to gulp food with little chewing; to desert or withdraw support from; to blurt impulsively. Can anyone tell me which of those things this character's eyes did?

Catch Those Eyes

Always apply the Find and Refine Method to your manuscript to find and replace any misuse of the word *eyes*.

I sometimes understand the intent of the flawed sentences I spot, but good English avoids ambiguity. I think you'll get a chuckle from the following Manu-slips, but while you smile, remember never to give agents or publishers an opportunity to laugh at your manuscript, except in the places where you intended to entertain.

- He stared at her for a moment, his eyes curling in a warm smile.
- John's eyes rose to meet hers.
- Even looking away, she saw his face and remembered every inch: his smiling eyes above thick brows, his square, determined jaw. [I cannot imagine brows under the eyes, but maybe you can.]
- Jim looked away to avoid his friend's eyes pinning him to the wall.
- The Italian captain had a craggy face, football nose, pure white teeth, and curly hair, surrounding brown eyes. [I don't know about you, but I would not want to meet a man whose face, nose, teeth, and hair all surrounded his eyes.]
- A blue-flowered brunch coat matched her eyes. [She had flowers in her eyes?]

- Her eyes rolled to the top of her head.
- Fear escaped through her eyes.
- Her eyes were wide, dark and dreamy. They never approached Sam, but rested quietly in the doorway.
- His eyes were enticed. They lapped at her knees and thighs.
- His eyes bounced around the barnyard.
- Her eyes fell on the children. [Imagine all the horrified children!]
- My eyes bored into hers.
- He transferred his eyes from the floor to the window.
- His eyes slid off of Max and glided over to a black speck dotting the white wall.
- He laughed as his eyes alternated from the sky to her face.
- With widened eyes, her hand moved to feel behind her. [As written, this dangling modifier implies that her hand had eyes.)
- Ricky's eyes roamed over the crowd.
- She caught Louis's eyes.
- Sal's eyes lazily wandered down into the valley past pine trees and wheat fields.
- Our eyes were drawn together like magnets.
- His eyes ran the gamut of the crowd.
- I kept my eyes glued to Pat's head.
- Four sets of eyes dropped to the floor. [Yuck!]
- Her eyes were frozen on the ground.
- The detectives' eyes locked together.
- His giddiness dies when Mary's eyes dive back into the newspaper.

13

PUT THE PEDAL TO THE METTLE

For this chapter I lifted items from columns I've written on the topic of creative writing. The subjects require thinking and decision-making on your part, instead of relying on your computer. It's your turn to show your mettle.

First, let's learn my convictions about revealing your opinions. Consider the ways you might air your beliefs without being obvious.

On Ego

Opinions are like rear ends; everyone has one, but no one wants to examine anyone else's. Does that premise mean we writers can never reveal our convictions? Absolutely not. We wouldn't have become writers, if we didn't have strong beliefs and weren't looking for ways to tell others about them, so let the opinions roll, with a few reservations.

What's a Writer to Do?

Let's say you are a starving writer and land an assignment that will pay the rent, but the magazine wants you to report on the value of electric-shock dog collars. You consider their use inhumane, but your rent is overdue. Do you swallow your pride and write a glowing report on the virtues of shocking helpless animals into submission? Do you refuse the job, knowing the next time you sit on your sofa, it will be on the curb? Do you beg for a different assignment?

We can't make a good decision without exploring all possibilities, and in every situation, many options exist, some we don't even know about. Instead of quitting your job or refusing an assignment you don't like, write the piece, but write a balanced piece. Interview any sources the publisher gives you, even if they manufacture and sell items you consider medieval torture devices. Round out the information with interviews of people who have used the product. Ask about drawbacks they've experienced. Chances are you'll get a few negatives to add to your article. Finally, call veterinarians and representatives of the Humane Society. You may frame your questions to get negative responses, or you may find their opinions make you change your mind. When you finish, you'll have a balanced article that allows readers to make up their own minds.

If you're a good writer, you can make a case against the product, yet still satisfy your publisher. Take the money and run to the bank. You've voiced your opinion through the mouths of others, and you've learned the value of balanced journalism.

The Ego Hypothesis Also Applies to Fiction

Many writers of fiction spout off personal opinions in their novels and short stories. Sometimes writers unconsciously use words in narrative that reflect their personal opinions. A few personal-opinion words that come to mind include the following: *obviously, hopefully, thankfully, incredible, beautiful, remarkable, awesome,* and *of course.* Editorializing in fiction is an absolute no-no, but do not dismay. Fiction writers have even more opportunity to seduce the reader with their own opinions, provided they do so through the voices of their characters.

Mary Contrary may be a minor character, yet she can tell her boyfriend in strong terms that she disapproves of his dog-training methods. She can say shocking dogs is cruel, while rewarding them for good behavior works better. Perhaps the story can show the police charging one of your characters with cruelty to animals for using a device that delivers an electric shock. The prosecution can mouth the words you would say, and your points will reach readers loud and clear.

Explore All Opportunities

Do writers have to park their egos at the door? No. We can write nonfiction, such as editorials, letters to the editor, and personal essays. In our fiction, we can quote other people who say what we want to say or create characters that voice our opinions for us.

Hey, we can even write articles for other writers and sneak in our opinions. I did, didn't I? As a result of reading this portion of my book, don't you now know how I feel about shock collars? I trust that through my examples, you learned how to air your beliefs without showing your briefs.

Without an ego, we can't have opinions. Ego, that little part of us that demands to be heard and craves to be right can fight, kick, and scream to make its point. Like our opinions, should our ego reveal itself in our writing? Read on.

Does Your Writing Need a Trip to the ER?

Ouch! Rejection hurts. How can we stem the flow of rejections?

Ego is a dangerous obstacle that can stand in the way of a manuscript sale. When you take your writing through Ego Removal (ER), you stand a better chance of getting it published.

Before you can perform an ego-ectomy, you must understand ego, why it works against you, and how to recognize it in your work.

Ego, as any psychiatrist will explain, is the part of our personality that always has to be right. To be right, the ego strives for recognition, and that's where danger lurks.

The old adage holds true: The customer is always right. Once you understand that you are the salesperson for your manuscript, not the customer, you'll see why you must remove your ego from the equation and let the customer win. You want to sell your manuscript, right?

Ego in Letters

Ego often multiplies like bacteria and infects our work. Examine this typical opening from many a cover letter or query letter:

Dear (agent or publisher):

I have just completed my first novel entitled *This Little Piggy Goes to Market.*

Repent, and send no more! Agents and publishers are busy people. Don't tell them what they already know. They assume you have written something, or you wouldn't be contacting them. You have also revealed deadly information. You've shown you'll waste their time telling the obvious, and that you are a first-time author. In addition, the use of *entitled* to mean *titled* is a variant, a gray area open to prejudice, just as the spelling of *grey* is a variant. Editors might assume (whether true or not) that you not only make errors in your work, but also, because "I" is the very first word in your letter, you're going to be a difficult client, a prima donna.

Stick to the tried and true. Be professional in your approach.

After removal of the ego, the letter becomes businesslike, direct, and without frills. It describes the product for sale, not you. Consider the following revision:

Dear (agent or publisher):

This Little Piggy Goes to Market is a 65,000-word psychological thriller set in Galway, Ireland, in the 1990s. Mary Pigson pens a novel. In her efforts to sell it, she learns the value of ego removal.

The letter doesn't have to be much longer. You are acting like a professional, so you will follow the agent's or publisher's guidelines diligently. As a result, the letter doesn't have to say you've enclosed a synopsis, SASE, three sample chapters, or anything else the guidelines told you to include. The letter doesn't even have to say you want to sell the book. Avoid the obvious facts. The letter should never say you live with your cat in California, unless the book is about your cat.

Yes, you will add a brief paragraph that includes your writing successes in the past, if you have had any, but otherwise, refer to the manuscript, rather than yourself.

Who Did You Say Is Always Right?

Let's return to pleasing your customer. When you go to the store to buy a car stereo, do you want to know the salesperson has a dog? You don't want to know how long the person has been in sales or that he or she has never before sold a car sound system. You care about the car stereo. You want to know its functions, availability, and cost. You don't care where the salesperson lives or how long he or she studied sales. Don't put such facts in your letter, either. Don't say how long you've studied writing or admit that you've never sold a manuscript or that you self-published your first novel.

When you remember you are in the business of selling your manuscript, you will remember to stick to business.

Now for the manuscript

Your auxiliary materials are only part of the ER approach. Examine the manuscript itself. Whenever an author feels the need to tell readers about a character's thoughts, background, or motivation, the author suffers from ego inflation.

Check every bit of narrative in the manuscript to see if it uses abstract adjectives that reflect the author's opinion. *Beautiful, wonderful, delightful, lovely, handsome, bleak, awesome, amazing, inspiring,* and most other abstract, rather than concrete, adjectives reveal what the author thinks, but they give little information to readers. Instead, use concrete adjectives, visual ones, and let readers form their own opinions.

Here's a sentence with the ego still intact: *Richard's lovely wife presented him with an expensive gift for his birthday.* Here is the same information written without personal opinion, ego: *Richard's wife flung back her curly hair and smiled at him with* *her golden-flecked eyes. She handed him a Rolex watch worth $15,000 and cooed, "Happy birthday."*

When you write a sentence that says *Mary was worried*, that's telling, rather than showing, and it's revealing what you as the writer know, instead of allowing readers to determine the truth for themselves. If you want readers to know Mary's emotional state, show it through her actions and dialogue, rather than through narrative from an ego-inflated author.

Thoughts—inner dialogues—are subtle ways for an author's ego to sneak into fiction. In real life, we cannot read people's thoughts. In our manuscripts, our ego wants to say, "Hey! I'm so right, so perfect, I can read minds." Don't give in to the urge.

Here's a passage with internal dialogue:

Stephen waited for the door to open and reveal his blind date. *She's not bad,* he thought. *A little round in the rump and an extra chin, but at fifty, what can I expect? I lost my hair twenty years ago, and my rear end isn't so small, either.*

Here's a possible revision without thoughts:

Stephen waited for the door to open and reveal his blind date. She stood before him, heavy in the rump and with a double chin, but her pleasant smile made him forget. He brushed his fiftyish hand over his balding head and sputtered, "Hi, I'm Stephen."

Avoid relying on thoughts to reveal the inner workings of your characters' minds. Instead, reveal their thoughts through their actions, responses, and conversations with other characters. You may even have to add another character to fulfill this requirement. I added a best friend to my first novel, to avoid getting into my main character's head too much. Instead of inner dialogue, or thoughts, the main character had a friend in whom she could confide. The revision enhanced my story.

Scrub Up and Cut Away

Study your manuscript, cover letter, and synopsis. Excise all vestiges of yourself and your ego. Focus on the story, and you'll have a more marketable manuscript. It'll hurt only a little, until you make your sale. When you receive your check, you can use it to buy bandages for your bruised ego or for a fine bottle of champagne to celebrate. I think you'll choose the champagne.

While we're on the subject of ego, which tells, rather than shows readers what you want them to know, let me delve deeper into the showing-versus-telling theory.

How Can I tell When I'm Telling?

A writer I know attended a writers conference and met with an agent who was seeking new clients. He pitched his story to the agent, and the agent asked for his manuscript. Excited, he handed over his entire 320-page baby. The agent scanned the first page, flipped through a few other pages, and shook her head. When she handed the manuscript back to the dismayed writer, the agent explained that his manuscript told, rather than showed, and it needed more work.

The writer complained to me that agent's words cut him to the core. He added, "I'm a good writer. If she'd read on, she would have seen all the action, twists, and turns. How could she say my story told, rather than showed? She only glanced at the first page and a few others."

I explained about poor, tired agents. Agents and publishers see hundreds of manuscripts a month, and they learn quick ways to detect whether a manuscript will interest them. I've already explained that publishers want mainstream fiction to unfold like a movie. To determine whether a story tells, rather than shows, one quick trick agents and others use is to check the percentage of dialogue. Fiction should be about seventy percent dialogue.

If the first page has little or no dialogue, a red flag goes up in an agent's mind, but most agents don't give up there. The next test determines how much of the narrative involves action— characters doing things, getting into plot-related, tension-inducing situations. If instead of action, the opening pages describe the scenery, the setting, or someone's physical description or background, it tells, rather than shows, and it needs rewriting.

Does the story begin with someone waking up? Another red flag. Publishers have grown weary of wake-up scenes as an opener. They consider wake-up scenes overused, time wasting, and fraught with insignificant action.

Contemporary fiction does not begin with static exposition or cliché situations. It jumps into the action. It hooks the reader with strong verbs that show activity, preferably gripping, interesting, plot-related action.

How can you tell if your narrative tells, rather than shows? Here's another quick trick: check how many times the narrative uses any form of the verb *to be*. More than about four or five on page one, and the manuscript tells, rather than shows. Page one is the beginning of a chapter. If you put your manuscript into correct format, the first page starts about a third of the way down the page. The writing exhibits weakness if it relies on four uses of the verb *to be* in only two-thirds of a page, especially that vital first page.

Agents and publishers rarely read beyond that first page, so the first page must be perfect. Dan Veach, editor and publisher of the internationally renowned literary publication *Atlanta Review*, once said, "I only have to read a manuscript until it becomes unpublishable." If the first page reveals itself to be unpublishable, editors assume the remainder to be the same. Their time is too valuable to waste, so they stop reading and reject the manuscript.

Find Your Flaws

Check your fiction manuscripts. If you want an agent or publisher to read past the first page, you must choose strong action verbs and write tight scenes that reveal people doing things that lead them somewhere, get them in trouble, create conflict, set them up for the next scene, or otherwise draw readers into your story. The entire book, and especially the first page, should move forward in that manner.

Let's say you want to make the following points in your opening: David is a writer; the setting is Savannah, Georgia; the month is August. Consider the following potential opening that tells:

The sun was hot and bright on that August morning in Savannah. No one was around on the public squares, but there were birds in the trees. The sun was shining in David's window when the writer decided to get up and start the day.

Here's a possible rewrite that shows a little more, rather than telling as much as the first example:

> The sun rose hot and bright through David's window on that August morning before the writer pried his eyes open. Although no people strolled through Savannah's public squares outside, birds sang in the trees. David stretched and swung his legs off the side of the bed.

Which is better? The second is an improvement. It does show more than it tells, but did you forget that one of the most overused openings is a wake-up scene? I'll bet you'll never forget it, now. An even better rewrite, then, might be this one:

> David pecked at his typewriter keys all night, until the August sun glared through his window. He stretched to bring life back into his body before he rose to gulp another cup of coffee. Outside, birds flitted about in the trees, but he heard no traffic sounds yet. Soon buses, taxis, cars, trolleys and even horse-drawn carts would trek around Savannah's public squares.

Agents and publishers look for action and dialogue, so if you added dialogue to the last revision, you would have an even better opening:

> David pecked at his typewriter keys all night, until the August sun glared through his window. He glanced at the clock. "Damn! Morning already?" He stretched to bring life back into his body before he rose to gulp another cup of caffeine. "Honey? Want any coffee?"

A snort and continued snores answered him from the bedroom.

Outside, birds flitted about in the trees, but he heard no traffic sounds yet. Soon buses, taxis, cars, trolleys and even horse-drawn carts would trek around Savannah's public squares.

Ah, but where is the hook? Why do readers care if David worked all night and his love interest is still sleeping? Here's perhaps the best way to open the same scene with action, dialogue, setting, and conflict:

David pecked at his typewriter keys all night, until the August sun glared through his window. He glanced at the clock. "Damn! Morning already?" He stretched to bring life back into his body before he rose to gulp another cup of caffeine. "Honey? Want any coffee?"

No answer came from the bedroom.

Outside, birds flitted about in the trees, but he heard no traffic sounds yet. Soon buses, taxis, cars, trolleys and even horse-drawn carts would trek around Savannah's public squares.

David called from the kitchen again. "Honey? Coffee's ready."

Again no one answered.

Hairs rose on the back of his neck. "Mike? Are you all right?" David slammed down his cup and raced to the bedroom.

What vital pieces of information did we get from the final revision? We now know that David is gay and something might be wrong with Mike. Do we want to read on to find out if Mike is okay? You bet we do.

When you feel compelled to set the scene or give background information, do it later, after page one, or intersperse the information with interesting action and conflict. You can't eliminate every instance of telling, rather than showing, but keep each occurrence short—no longer than a brief paragraph here and there—interspersed with action and dialogue, and the manuscript will stand a better chance of catching the eye of readers, agents, and publishers.

The above information on showing rather than telling refers primarily to fiction, but you can improve your nonfiction articles and books using similar techniques. To show rather than tell a nonfiction story, add anecdotes and examples. They allow you to add dialogue and action.

Does Your Manuscript Need a Haircut?

Whew! I finished editing a book for a publisher in Washington, D.C., and the job took much longer than usual. The author had a marketable subject and the writing skills to interest a traditional publisher, but the book still had to be edited by a professional. To give you an idea of what professional editors do, I'll let you peep into the mistakes I found in that otherwise publishable manuscript.

First I addressed inconsistencies. In one place, the book referred to party favors as goody bags. The term is acceptable, but later on, the manuscript refers to goodie bags. Whoops! Either *goody* or *goodie* is correct, but a manuscript must be consistent.

Sometimes the author capitalized the names of committees, and at other times did not. Pick one choice and stick to it.

One Word or Two?

Perhaps the second-most corrected errors I've made centered on words that could be one word, two, or hyphenated. The same held true for the manuscript I am discussing. Computers don't pick up every one of those mistakes, because often the words are right, whether they stand together or apart. Only a professional human eye can catch the difference. As an example, here are only a few of the words in that manuscript that were written as two words, but that should have been one: *afterthought, mealtime, pastureland, peacemaking, lunchtime, loudspeaker, clockwork, mindset, lighthearted, heavyset, brokenhearted, treetop,* and *newfound.*

Did you put those words into your computer and find that the spell-checker told you to break them into two words? Ha! That's because spell-checking programs are not the final authority. Use them as guides. Only a careful editor or a good dictionary can discern the truth, and because dictionaries differ, book publishers usually prefer *Merriam-Webster*

Pronoun Clarity

Above all else, writers must strive for clarity. To ensure clarity, and to follow correct rules of grammar, a pronoun cannot be too far away from the noun it reflects. Ponder this sentence: *Three men unrolled their prayer rugs, and after they spread out, they sat down.*

Readers may not clearly know whether the men spread out or the rugs spread out. For clarity, you might rewrite the sentence this way: *Three men unrolled prayer rugs, spread them out, and sat down.*

Also for clarity, the pronoun should not precede the noun. For example, instead of a sentence like this: *As he grabbed Jill's hand, Barry winked.* Clearer would be this: *As Barry grabbed Jill's hand, he winked.*

Such flaws don't look all that bad, do they? After all, some of the above examples came from a manuscript that the author had sold to a traditional publisher. The publisher knew the manuscript needed the critical eye and careful hand of a professional editor, though, which is why he engaged my services before publishing the book.

We Know What We Mean

When we write, we all know what we mean to say, and we feel confident we said what we meant. Why, then, do mistakes creep in? Because we can't see our own errors. We're too close to them. I received an e-zine from a reputable source, and in one column, an author veered from the original subject, and to get back to the subject at hand, he wrote, *But I digest . . .* I didn't even know he was hungry. He knew he meant to say that he *digressed,* though, and he thought that was what he said. Every writer who ever put ink on paper has made similar mistakes that only another person can catch. Thank goodness for this universal truth, or we editors could not have had the great careers that we've had.

The Big Question

Should you use a professional editor? Asking me that question is like asking a barber if you need a haircut.

Here's my answer, though. Using another pair of eyes always takes time and sometimes costs you money, but will you miss the money or time if your manuscript gets accepted and published? No, you will only look at your success.

On the other hand, will you make money or get published by rushing your manuscript to agents and publishers while it is still in rough form? Rarely. Few want to work with coal; they want diamonds. Will you gain credentials and prestige if you self-publish a book teeming with errors? No. You will only lose face and waste your time and money.

Look at your goals and do whatever it takes to reach them. If you want to sell your work, get someone else to edit your manuscript; you cannot do it yourself.

Do you have to hire a professional? No, not if you have a good critique circle filled with experts familiar with Chicago style and able to spot and repair the flaws you cannot see. You also may not need to pay a professional if you have a knowledgeable friend willing to edit your book for you.

Spend the time, if not the money. Get the "haircut" that makes your manuscript ready to meet the public.

14

BOBBIE'S BILL OF WRITES

When I speak to writers one-on-one, at times I sense their angst. Some feel embarrassed to admit they are writers, as if being a writer were a disease best left undisclosed. Some fear revealing their penchant for writing because they have not yet been published. Others have other reasons for not saying they are writers.

Years ago I set out to overcome the reluctance of writers to show pride in their craft. At my workshops and meetings, I require attendees to introduce themselves and say, "I am a writer." I hand out name tags at meetings of The Writers Network, and the name tags say, "Hi, I'm . . . and I'm a writer."

When I was a member of the board of trustees for the Georgia Writers Association for many years, I instituted the same requirement. In every networking session, each person stood, introduced himself or herself, and added, "and I am a writer."

We writers must believe in ourselves; if not, who will believe in us? We must take pride in our work. We must demand the respect that is rightfully ours. No longer should we be reluctant to admit we are writers. An old Talmudic saying goes, "If I'm not for me, who will be?"

Some folks think they can't call themselves writers until they sell or publish something. How can they sell or publish their work, though, until they first write it? How can they write it, without being writers?

For validation, you do not need to be a published or paid writer. To be a writer, you need only to write.

Let me repeat myself: To be a writer, you need only to write.

If you don't feel worthy to call yourself a writer or to demand whatever you need to become an accomplished writer, Bobbie's Bill of Writes is for you. Heck, even accomplished writers need my Bill of Writes.

First I will give you the list. Photocopy it and hang in a prominent spot in your working space. After the list I will go into detail on each subject.

Bobbie's Bill of Writes

As a writer, you have the right to do the following:

1. Call yourself a writer.
2. Spend the money and time necessary to improve your craft.
3. Spend time alone practicing your craft.
4. Have a place where you can write.
5. Buy the equipment you need or want.
6. Set goals.
7. Tell others about your successes.
8. Wander starry-eyed through an office supply store.
9. Spend time "doing nothing."
10. Take a vacation from writing—with a predetermined end date.
11. Spend money and time sending submissions.
12. Feel sad—for a specified length of time.
13. Get help if you feel depressed.

14. Celebrate each milestone.
15. Create a schedule and stick to it.
16. Use a thesaurus.
17. Demand respect for your chosen craft.
18. Get feedback on your work.
19. Ignore unworthy advice.
20. Make mistakes.
21. Other and further relief.

Bobbie's Bill of Wrongs

As a writer, you do *not* have the right to do the following:

1. Be defensive.
2. Delay your work for unworthy reasons.
3. Avoid your obligation to spread knowledge.
4. Say harmful things to other writers.
5. Devote energy to your rejection slips.
6. Avoid submitting work for fear of rejection.
7. Take rejection personally.
8. Dull your senses.

Let that list be your reminder of all the details I am about to impart.

You Have the Right to: Call Yourself a Writer

Have you ever read a self-help book or attended a motivational event? If so, you know you have to believe something before you can manifest it. Once you believe you are a writer, you will write, practice, learn, and hone your craft until you become successful in whatever way you define success. I urge all writers to say "I am a writer" and say it with pride and conviction.

Writers tell me they are reluctant to admit they are writers, for fear that someone will say, "Really? What have you sold? Have I read anything you wrote?"

Writers do not have to publish to be writers. If we use a pen or sit at a keyboard and type, we are writers.

Plan ahead. Practice your answer. The next time someone asks what you do, answer with pride. Your answer might be, "I sell life insurance for Acme Mutual, I run a household, and I write children's books." It might be "I am a husband, a father, a poet, and a paramedic." My answer is this: "I am the owner of Zebra Communications, a book-editing firm, and I write books about creative writing."

If someone asks if you have sold anything, answer with a positive, such as this: "I'm working on it." Your answer also may go like this: "My letter to the editor appeared in the *Metro Times* last month." You do not have to say you received no pay for it. Word your answer in a way that gives you the pride and sense of accomplishment you deserve. Practice your answers until you feel comfortable saying them.

You Have the Right to: Spend the Money and Time Necessary to Improve Your Craft

You have the right to improve your craft, and improvement requires time and money. Whenever you ponder whether you should buy a book, take a course, join an organization, subscribe to a magazine, or attend a conference, do it. If you have an interest in writing, you have the right to pursue it.

You may find that many expenses are deductible, if you plan to sell your writing. Check with your accountant or the person who prepares your taxes and enjoy the surprise when you find out you can do many things you never thought possible and deduct all or part of the cost. As an example, I used Frequent Flyer miles to fly to Ireland in 2002. Once there, I took a ground tour with my sister and her husband, along with about a dozen other people. We had a blast. I came home and sold one article based on the trip and wrote three other free articles that were published in newsletters for writers. My accountant allowed me to deduct almost half the cost of the trip. When you add back in what I got paid for the one consumer-magazine article, my trip cost me about a quarter of the actual cost.

You Have the Right to: Spend Time Alone Practicing Your Craft

No one lives in isolation. You have many demands on your time. Parents, siblings, significant others, even animals and friends make demands on you. In addition, you may have to spend time at work, at school, and on the road going to and from work or school. You wash your clothes, clean your abode, feed yourself, and even relax or meditate. I hope you also spend time working out or exercising in some way. You are not alone in wondering when you will ever find time to write, especially when the people you love want to spend time with you and you have so many other tasks and demands.

You must spend time alone, though, or you will never write. No one has ever written a great work of art at a family reunion, although a family reunion can certainly provide great material.

Life will make demands on your time; that's a known fact. Your only defense is to make a schedule, stick to it, and write without interruption at least once a week. Trust me, you will never *find* the time to write. You must *make* the time to write. Make it a priority. Do whatever it takes to create the time you need to practice your craft.

You Have the Right to: Have a Place Where You Can Write

When I was young, I envied Mother her little office nook in the kitchen, a desk loaded with cubbyholes. In her space she could talk on the phone, pay bills, spread paper out, write, or do whatever she saw fit.

Daddy had a desk in the bedroom, and I envied him that piece of furniture, where he could sit at his manual typewriter and strike keys with concentration. I longed to own a desk like his.

As an adult, I have created several spaces where I feel comfortable, where I can write. You too deserve a location that is all yours, a retreat or cave of your own.

What and where are your spaces? If you do not have a space, make one today. Let it be sacred, all yours, a place where you can write in peace and comfort. Ideally it should be a place where you can spread out your work and leave it, without having to clear it off for company or family use.

You Have the Right to: Buy the Equipment You Want

I bought a sturdy Mac desktop computer when I founded my business in 1992, and it ran well and served me faithfully for many years. Technology advanced, though, and after a while I had an urge to own a laptop too.

Logic held me back, though. Instead of being decisive, I spent months researching, wavering, studying brands, considering their advantages and disadvantages, procrastinating, and trying to justify the purchase. Still, I did not buy a laptop until I walked into an office supply store one day, saw a PC laptop at a reduced rate, and bought it on the spur of the moment.

At first I played games on my new toy. I had little other use for it. Soon I found that when clients sent me PC disks I could easily work on them with my PC laptop. I did not have to convert the files to Mac and convert them back to PC files when I finished. One sizable project performed on the laptop paid for the new equipment.

When the beach called, I carried my laptop and mingled work with pleasure. Months later, I took my laptop to Australia and spent a month there while I wrote the book proposal for this book and maintained my business by e-mail. Way back then I had to dial up to connect to the Internet, but things have gotten even easier now.

When I later broke my leg, instead of closing down my business, I was able to work on my laptop, even though I could not go down the stairs to reach my office. Today I am on my third or fourth laptop, but it stays on, and I have two offices in my house—one upstairs and one downstairs.

I know it's time to get a tablet, as well, and I will get one soon, to make traveling even easier.

You never know when you will need equipment. Follow your urges and buy what you want, and soon you will need it or find uses for it. You have the right to buy equipment that makes your life easier, more pleasant, and more successful.

You Have the Right to: Set Goals

You must know your goals, if you expect to reach them. Yes, you might like to write, but what result do you hope to achieve?

Earlier in this book I asked you to think of why you write. If you did not do it then, please do it now. Write down all the ways you define success. You may have one or more of the following goals: to chronicle your life or your family history, pass along the information you have gained in your life, make money, change careers, record the stories in your head, or gain new clients for your business. You may have another goal I have not even mentioned, but only you can know why you write and how you define success with your writing.

To reach your goal, you must have more than a vague idea of what it is. Take pen in hand and write down your exact goal or goals. Next decide when you want to achieve them. Do you want to change careers within three years? Write down today's date, your goal, and its deadline three years from today.

Do you want to sell your short stories? Define your goals, write them down, and set dates by which you want to achieve them.

Post your goals prominently in your office or carry them in your wallet, but look at them often, and you are on your way to achieving them.

You may accelerate your schedule with the use of affirmations. An affirmation is a short sentence that states your goal as if you have already reached it, as if it is happening as you speak. An affirmation is something declared to be true. Your affirmation may look like some of these: *I sell my novel to a major publisher. My nonfiction book wins a national award. My speeches get quoted in the newspaper. I sell articles to consumer magazines with a circulation of 100,000 and above.* Your affirmation can be as specific as you want.

Here are some other possible affirmations that may help you write your own:

- I write children's books that get published in America as well as other countries.
- I sell fifteen feature articles to trade publications each year.
- Twice a month I write proposals that bring new business to my company.

- I write one novel every year and sell it for advances of $15,000 plus royalties of 6% of retail.
- I write poems that bring out emotions in others.
- I write nonfiction books that teach others how to be successful, and I complete a new book every three years.

Write down your affirmation. Sign it, date it, and display it in a prominent spot in your work space. Read it and repeat it many times every day. The more you repeat your affirmation, the quicker it will come true. Believe it, and you will achieve it.

Because I have many deadlines looming at all times, I used to feel panic creeping into my life. I get less done when I panic, plus I harm my body. Panic strangles me and tightens the muscles in my back and shoulders. Sometimes it gives me stomach cramps. I get less done, just when I need to do the most. I learned a perfect affirmation that gets me through those tough times, and I use it often. It goes like this: *I have enough time, energy, and wisdom to accomplish all my tasks.* When I feel stress coming on from my busy workload, I say to myself over and over, "I have enough time, energy, and wisdom to accomplish all my tasks." Whenever I do, my stress dissipates, and voilà, I do accomplish all my tasks.

You Have the Right to: Tell Others About Your Successes

Why on God's green earth does success create shyness in some people? Are they afraid if they boast, others will consider them braggarts? Do they fear their achievement won't be as great as someone else's? Why else do we write, if not to achieve success, and what good is success if no one knows about it?

Promise me and promise yourself that from this day forward, when your poem appears on an Internet site, when you have an op-ed piece published in the paper, when you write a manual that makes life simpler for someone else, or when whatever you write gets published in print or on the Internet, regardless of whether you get paid, you will tell others about your successes. Be sure to write up your successes and send them to your social and professional organizations for inclusion in their newsletters, websites, and e-zines. Post your successes on your Facebook page. Tweet about them on Twitter. Use all the forms of social media available to you to let the world know about your success. Enjoy the praise you receive.

I lead a group called The Writers Network. Besides disseminating information to writers, it also gives them a forum to announce their successes. At the back of this book, read how you can join my free network and receive my free monthly e-zine, *The Writers Network News*.

Success breeds success. The more you talk about success, the more you succeed. Your successes not only drive you forward, but they also encourage others to succeed.

You Have the Right to: Wander Starry-Eyed Through an Office Supply Store

Julia Cameron, who wrote *The Artist's Way*, recommends that artists make dates with themselves to do whatever makes them feel like artists. When I heard about that idea, I knew my artist's date would be at an office supply store, where I could pore over the stationery, binders, folders, erasers, stickers, rubber stamps, gizmos, gadgets, and you name it. I like colorful file folders and multicolored paper clips, especially.

Some supplies improve my efficiency and others increase my pleasure as I work. Granted, some sit in a drawer waiting for me to find a use for them. So what?

As a writer, you are also an artist. Let the artist in you come out to play, to find the tools and toys that make you a more contented writer.

You Have the Right to: Spend Time "Doing Nothing"

Most of us know that the alpha state, the one in which we are first falling asleep, is the one where inventors, songwriters, and writers access their most brilliant thoughts. I've heard that Thomas Edison took little naps during the day, and although he may not have known what to call his technique, he intentionally accessed his alpha state for solutions and new ideas.

Our brains are never quiet, but we cannot always hear what our brains have to say, when our bodies are busy. To access your endless imagination, your inventive state, all you must do is "do nothing." I put the phrase in quotation marks, because even when we seem to be doing nothing, our minds continue to work, and when we are in a quiet state, we can hear our thoughts and tap into our creativity.

You may choose to take power naps of twenty minutes or less, as Edison did, or you may meditate or sit still in a relaxed position and let your mind wander.

I meditate. I may not be as consistent as some folks are, but when I am not rushed to meet an appointment in the morning, I have a routine that works wonders for me. Before I get out of bed, I take a deep breath and let it out slowly, making the sound of "Ah-h-h-h." I continue deep breathing and sound repetition until my body relaxes. In a meditative state, I visualize the way I want my day to go, what I want to bring into my life, what I will achieve that day. I "see" me accomplishing the tasks on my list. The few minutes of meditation allow me to plan my day and see it unfold the way I want. I love the joy of starting each day with a meditation before I stretch and get out of bed.

In the evenings before I fall asleep, I meditate again, this time making the sound of "Om-m-m-m" when I exhale. In the meditative state, I give thanks for all the gifts and joys of the day, for all the loving people in my life, and for the privilege of doing what I want, to make my living. I mentally express gratitude for all the good things in my life.

True, I do not produce anything tangible during those times I "do nothing," but I let my body relax, so the brain can go out to play.

When I took a course in Silva Mind Development and Stress Control, I learned a different way to meditate, although the deep breathing is consistent throughout any form of meditation. With Silva, I learned to count backwards to myself with each deep breath. "Ten, ten, ten." Next breath: "Nine, nine, nine," and so forth, until I reached one, by which time I was in a meditative state.

Intentionally reach the alpha state often, and your tension reduces and creativity increases, but meditation is not the only way to achieve the alpha state. You can also stare out a window or lean back in an easy chair and look at the ceiling. Your mind travels freely when your body relaxes.

Don't forget to keep paper and pen nearby to write down ideas, titles, dialogue, or other thoughts that come to you as you float through a delightful, restful alpha state.

You Have the Right to: Take a Vacation From Writing— with a Predetermined End Date

Treat writing as your career, even if it is part-time, because if you treat it as a hobby, it will remain one. Make no mistake about it; writing is work, even when it brings you joy. To refresh your mind and keep you in a creative state, you must take time off from your regular work, whatever it is, and you must take time off from writing, too. Writing requires self-disciple, and it requires rest. Do not feel guilty when you take a vacation from writing, but do set an ending date for your holiday, and stick to it.

Writers may find themselves in family crises or other situations that distract them from writing. If something diverts your attention, set an end date for when your furlough from writing will end. Give yourself the hiatus you need. If, for example, you have a new baby, decide to return to your writing when the baby turns three months old.

We cannot predict the future, though. If your mother's health has taken a downturn and she needs you by her side, you may not know how long you will be away from your writing. In such a case, set a situation-specific end date, such as this one: "When I am no longer needed to take care of Mother for three or more hours a day, I will return to my writing." Such an end date allows for any turn of events.

Allow yourself the freedom you need, so that writing does not become a chore. It should never be the thing you put off for all your other responsibilities. Writing *is* a responsibility.

You Have the Right to: Spend Money and Time Sending Submissions

Every job has its good parts and its less-appealing ones. Let's imagine you have a job as a store manager and love to greet customers, but hate ordering supplies. If you diligently said hello to customers but avoided the paperwork necessary to order new inventory, your store soon would be out of goods and out of business. You would have no customers to greet. You kill the good part of a job if you do not tend to the parts you do not like.

The same is true of writing. The act of writing is only one part of our job. We must edit, rewrite, and submit our work. To submit it, writers must research their markets; follow guidelines; sometimes make copies; sometimes create self-addressed, stamped envelopes and sometimes prepare e-mails; write cover or query letters; sometimes take the packages to the post office; keep track our submissions; and always look for more markets. No matter what you write, you also have work that has nothing to do with writing. To see your work reach the public, you cannot be stingy with your time or money.

If you hate the editing, rewriting, or submissions part, pay for professional help. Some companies research markets, locate guidelines, and submit manuscripts to agents and publishers. Some websites claim to reach agents or publishers with submissions posted on their sites. Many companies and individuals edit manuscripts. My company is not the only one that provides editing services, although—pardon my pride—we are one of the best.

Look around, ask around, and get help with the tasks you hate. You may have to pay for the service, but you can get back to the parts of writing you prefer, without ignoring the other parts.

You Have the Right to: Feel Sad—for a Specified Length of Time

Must writers suffer? Everyone has moments of suffering; writers, however, turn those experiences into literature. The fact that writers suffer, though, does not mean we have to drink to excess or self-destruct in other ways.

While we learned to walk, we sometimes lost our balance and fell down, but we kept getting up and trying again, until we mastered the art of ambulating. When we send out our precious babies, our manuscripts, we must accept that we will sometimes fail—we will fall down—but we must get up and try again and again. Rejection is a part of our lives as writers, but it does not mean we will never get published, just as falling down did not mean we would never walk.

When we locate a market for our short story and get a "nice" rejection letter that says our story is almost good enough, but not quite ready for that magazine, it hurts. We must admit we hurt, admit that we feel sad, and shake it off.

Shaking it off can be as simple as shuddering, shaking our head, and then barging forward once again. My son learned this process when he played soccer, as early as nine years old. If a ball got past him and the other team scored a goal, he had to shake it off and get back in the game with the same enthusiasm he had before. We can certainly learn to do the same as adults.

Set your own statute of limitations. I allow myself three hours to feel bad, whenever I get another rejection for my work. After years in the trenches, I rarely need all three hours anymore, though. I have gotten adept at moving on. Some of the rejections have been big ones, too, such as the time I thought I had sold a magazine article to a new market I wanted to reach, but in the end, someone nixed it. I mumbled a few words that I won't repeat here, and I moved on. Did it hurt? Yes. Did I dwell on it? No. Today I can't even recall the name of that publication, but it's no longer in business. I lasted longer than it did.

When you receive a rejection letter, see it as an opportunity to reread your submission. Before you send the same submission to another publication, reread your work. If you spot ways to improve it, rewrite it. If you can find nothing to make it stronger, submit it elsewhere as is.

One of the best ways to avoid dwelling on rejection is to have several items out at once. When one comes back rejected, you have others still out there, so you have hope. Each rejection means you can send that piece to the next market and keep it circulating. Feel sad, but keep submitting manuscripts, and soon you'll feel fine again.

You Have the Right to: Get Help If You Feel Depressed

When I was in my late forties, several life stressors piled on me at once. Some were mental; some were physical. Some were internal; some were external. Some were environmental; some were self-made. I had sold my house and moved to a new city, started a new business, gotten engaged, found my relationship floundering, was going through menopause, and you name it. Stressors—not just bad events, but good ones, too—pile up, and if too many happen in too short a time, a person can become ill. Even though I knew about the ill effects of stressors, I could not stop my downward spiral.

Previously when I felt blue, I rose to my usual level of positive thinking within a day or two and moved on. That time, though, things grew worse by the day. I no longer wanted to get up in the morning. I forced myself out of bed, only to find myself lying on the sofa within a couple of hours. After about a month of being immobilized, I came to a realization: "I'm not sad, I'm depressed." I visited my doctor, who put me on antidepressants, and within weeks I was functioning at my normal level. Less than a year later, my business was up and running, my relationship had ended, but at least it had closure, and I had adjusted to living in a new city. I felt fine. I asked my doctor to take me off the medication, and the transition worked well. I have not needed antidepressants again, but I was thankful for the counseling and medication that saw me through a storm.

Recognize the difference between being a little blue and being chemically depressed. Get help when you need it, and be thankful it is available. I'm not proud of what I went through, but I'm not ashamed, because I took control and overcame it.

You Have the Right to: Celebrate Each Milestone

To celebrate a milestone, we must first understand them. Milestones are the markers, benchmarks that indicate we are moving forward.

What might be a milestone for a writer? When you conceive the idea for a new story, book, or article, you have started your journey. Consider conception your first mile marker. Celebrate! If you have a project assigned to you, make the first call, start your research, write the title of the project, or do whatever begins a new project, you have set your benchmark. From then on, celebrate each step that takes you closer to your goal.

You might celebrate the completion of your table of contents, which outlines the chapters you plan to write. You might celebrate making a list of contacts. If you write an outline, that's a marker. If you write a proposal and finish it, that's worthy of celebration. Honor each step, chapter, or activity that draws you closer to your goal. Celebrations lift our spirits and give us strength to continue.

Decide before you begin your project how you plan to celebrate each milestone and how you will celebrate completion of the project.

One of my writer friends finished the first draft of her nonfiction book, and to mark the occasion she invited friends to a celebration at a charming restaurant. The observance cost her nothing; we all paid for our own meals. Some folks even brought her little gifts to celebrate the milestone: pencils, pens, dark glasses and a hat, so she could go incognito when she becomes famous. She gave a brief speech thanking us for our support, and we cheered her and encouraged her to move on to the editing phase. Everyone had a good time, and she marked her milestone with grace.

When I came to an agreement with a publisher on publishing this book, I bought party favors that roll out and squeal when blown. Whenever I thought about all I had accomplished to have struck a deal with a reputable publisher, I pulled out my party favor and blew it. When I announced at a writers meeting that I had struck a deal with the publisher, I blew my party favor, everyone laughed, and I felt great. When the contract arrived in the mail, I blew my party favor, and my dog jumped around with excitement, thrilled about the noise. She celebrated my milestone with me.

You deserve to feel great. Once you identify your milestones, find ways to celebrate each one, and by all means, do so. You have the right!

You Have the Right to: Create a Schedule and Stick to It

"I'd love to write, but I don't have the time." That excuse does not work in my world. We all have the same number of hours each day, so how do some writers create a book in a year and others whine about not having the time?

We make time for things that matter to us. If your relationship matters, you find time to spend with your significant other. If school matters, you make time to study. If writing matters, make time to write.

Even if you don't think you plan your days, you do have patterns. You wake up at a certain time, eat meals at certain times, watch television at certain times, and take care of other responsibilities, as well. If writing is important to you, add it into your daily activities.

At one point in my busy life I made Thursday evenings my writing time. Friends and family members knew not to call me or invite me out on a Thursday night. I recorded the television programs I wanted to watch, and I got to work. I picked Thursday, because I had my critique circle every Saturday morning. I could write on Thursday night, let my pages rest overnight, reread them the next day, revise them, copy them, and be ready for my critique circle Saturday.

Your schedule should not only be a daily or weekly writing plan, but also one that depicts when you will finish certain projects. Deadlines motivate people.

When I give myself a deadline, I get the work done by breaking it into smaller tasks. If you want to finish your book in ten months and predict you'll have ten chapters, write one chapter a month. Schedule it in your daily planner, perhaps this way: On the last day of each month, write, "Finish chapter." On the first of each month, write "begin new chapter." On the date ten months away, write, "Finish book." Write it down, see your goals in writing, and you will meet them. Schedule your time and reap the benefits.

You Have the Right to: Use a Thesaurus

A thesaurus adds variety to your writing. When someone points out your tendency to overuse favorite words, use the thesaurus program on your computer or flip through a printed thesaurus and look up appropriate synonyms.

While some purists thumb their noses at the use of a thesaurus or consider it a form of cheating, wise writers who want to improve their style understand the value of a thesaurus. They turn to a thesaurus to find words they would have used, had they thought of them. Use your thesaurus as a memory trigger.

Don't use the thesaurus to find highfalutin words you would never say in conversation, though. Choose words that roll off your narrator's or character's tongue naturally, words you and your readers would not have to look up in a dictionary.

Here's another precaution about using a thesaurus: not every word in the list has the same definition as the word you looked up. Choose only the perfect words with the perfect connotations. Look up their meanings, if you are not certain of their connotations.

One of my favorite books is *Roget's International Thesaurus* (Thomas Y. Crowell Company), which my father gave me for graduation from high school back in the 1960s. That resourceful old book shows its wear and has been a valuable asset to me through the decades. Today writers also have the ease of an electronic thesaurus built into our software programs. The electronic thesaurus on my computer has a limited vocabulary, though. If it can't provide me with the exact word that's on the tip of my tongue, I lick my fingers and duck back into my printed thesaurus, which lists many more possibilities. Merrian-Webster.com also has a thesaurus online, for those who prefer electronics over printed pages.

You Have the Right to: Demand Respect for Your Chosen Craft

When I wrote advertising copy, I discovered that people sometimes asked me, "How are you doing on that little brochure you were writing?" Some said, "Did your client like the cute little commercial you wrote?" Although they may have thought they were flattering me with their interest, their comments annoyed me, but I could not put my finger on why. It finally struck me. By referring to my writing projects as "little," they were belittling my work. Although some of my projects paid less than others or took less time, none of them have been little to me. They all have importance; they have equal value.

I learned to answer in a way that demanded respect for my work, but I always said it with a smile. I might say, "That brochure isn't little. It's important to my client and to me." When appropriate, I responded, "That commercial isn't little. It's raking in money for my client."

An associate of mine told me an in-law of hers said, "Isn't it nice that your husband supports your little hobby?" My associate's "little hobby" landed her a good contract with a traditional publisher, and her first novel won three awards; two national, and one statewide. She won Georgia Author of the Year for First Novel, and the book was a BookSense 76 pick. It was nominated for the Townsend Award, too. My friend cringed when she heard the words "little hobby," but she has a better comeback now, should anyone ever again use demeaning words to refer to her successful writing career.

No one asks me how my "little" projects are going anymore. Once you teach others how to treat you and your craft, they respect what you do.

You Have the Right to: Get Feedback on Your Work

Feedback is essential to a writer, because we get too close to our own work. We think we know what we said. Only another person can be objective about your work. Others can see flaws, errors, repetition, or inconsistencies you might miss. Find or form a critique circle composed of people whose opinions you respect. Find an editor you trust. Get feedback on your work, and your writing will grow by leaps and bounds.

If you want to get free feedback or form a critique circle, attend meetings of writing organizations in your town and ask around. Don't be afraid to announce you are looking for critique partners; many others are looking, too. My website offers a free report on how to form a critique circle using all the techniques I perfected over the years. See http://zebraeditor. com/free_reports.shtml.

You can even make an announcement on the Internet that you are looking for critique partners, preferably in your genre. Look up websites for writers and ask for assistance in return for your reading the work of others. Critique circles are priceless, because you learn from others and also learn when you help others.

You Have the Right to: Ignore Unworthy Advice

I love this basic writer's right. You will be bombarded with advice. Sometimes you will even ask for it, as from an editor or a critique partner.

Nature instilled in us a stomach for more than one reason, though. Not only will your gut tell you when to eat, it will also tell you when to listen to advice. Your gut gives you the wisest counsel. Heed what it tells you. When someone says your point of view is all wrong in your story, listen to what he or she has to say. If the person has a credible reason why you should go to the trouble of changing the point of view, do so. If your gut grinds when you hear that person telling you what to change, though, don't do it. If several people tell you to change it, you might want to rethink your decision, but one person's advice is not enough to make major changes that go against what your instinct tells you.

Good friends with good intentions have told me entire books that I ought to write. I tell them the idea is good, and they should write it. My gut says I must write my own books, the ones that cry out to me, beg me to write them, and fuel my passion.

Weigh all advice and make your own decisions. Yes, you might not even listen to me and all that I say in this book. Great writers, after they have mastered the rules, create their own style and break out of the mold. Follow your heart and your gut, and you will do your best.

You Have the Right to: Make Mistakes

Human beings make mistakes; mistakes make us human. Everyone makes mistakes. Servers in restaurants sometimes get orders mixed up. Chefs sometimes overcook or under-season food. Mothers sometimes blame the wrong child for something that another child did. Bosses sometimes credit the wrong employee for a job another employee did. Lawyers make mistakes. Teachers make mistakes. Mathematicians make mistakes. Doctors make mistakes, and writers make mistakes. Mistakes are part of human nature.

When mistakes creep into print, though, we writers cringe and want to hide, as if we were the only ones ever to overlook something, yet every time we type a single character into our computer, we have the chance to make a slip-up. Every sentence gives us a chance to make another boo-boo. Each time we revise a word, sentence, paragraph, or chapter, we open ourselves up to a potential blunder.

While we have the right to make mistakes, strong writers do all they can to catch those gaffes before submitting a manuscript for publication. For that reason wise writers use personal diligence, but we need outside help, too. We do not know what we don't know, plus we are too close to our work. For those reasons, astute writers use critique circles and professional editors to double-check their manuscripts.

You Have the Right to: Other and Further Relief

I learned the legal term "other and further relief" when I took a brief job with an attorney's office in 1966. I fell in love with the vagueness of that term. I interpreted it to mean "anything more that you might be able to get."

I've added the term to my Bill of Writes because you may want other and further relief or guidance or goodies that I haven't listed, and you have the right to create your own rights.

You Do Not Have the Right to: Be Defensive

In my critique circles, we do not listen to writers defending their work. It wastes everyone's time. When someone gets defensive, my pat answer is, "Obviously it didn't work, or we would not advise you to change it. Only you can decide whether to change it, and we don't need to know if you did or didn't."

Years ago, an associate whose writing had faced much rejection shared his work with me. In the narrative, he had used the word *irregardless*, which blends two legitimate words, *regardless* and *irrespective,* into one substandard word. I explained that he could use the word in dialogue to show someone's ignorance, but in narrative he had to choose *regardless* or *irrespective.* He surprised me when he shook his head and said, "I thought about it, and I chose that word intentionally." His answer struck me as so odd that I didn't ask him why he would choose to show his own ignorance. Instead I never again gave him any feedback. He wanted only praise, not correction. His defense proved that I had wasted my time, so I never gave him advice again.

When you make a commitment to writing, it requires a commitment to learn more, and we can learn much from others. Even so, you have the right to ignore advice, so instead of defending your work, make notes on what people tell you, go home, think about it, look it up, and decide what you want to change and what you want to leave. Don't waste energy and time defending your work; use that time and energy to learn and create.

What if you're right? Good question. If you can answer someone with, "I looked it up and know it's right," that's not defending your work; that's informing the other person of the truth.

You Do Not Have the Right to: Delay Your Work for Unworthy Reasons

Some say writer's block is a myth perpetuated by the lazy. Don't listen to labels. Listen to yourself. You may procrastinate; we all do, but don't call it writer's block, or you may stay in that cradle of deception and never crawl out again. When you don't feel like writing, when you wash your dishes, paint your house, or plant your garden instead of writing your novel, call it what it is, a delaying tactic, and get your butt back into your chair and write.

I get e-mail notes from my sister Jean, who lives in Australia. At times she lists all the things she has to do and completes the list with this: "So naturally, I'm writing to you, instead." Her comment always tickles me because of its honesty, but in truth she also has accomplished great things in her life, including getting several college degrees and becoming an ordained minister.

You call yourself a writer, so have more than one project going at all times. If you cannot write on one project, write on another. Yes, you can procrastinate on one writing project to write a different one, and you're still writing.

Poetry always gets me over my procrastination. If I have no idea of what I want to write, I read a few poems, and soon my mind takes off on its own. Everything becomes a poem. A leaf floats down on my deck; I see it dancing in its death throes, and a poem emerges. At least I have written something.

When you are not sure what you want to write, you may delay sitting down to your computer, so keep a notebook of ideas. When your computer screen seems painfully blank, flip through your notebook, and one of your ideas will speak to you. Soon you'll be off and writing again.

Deadlines keep me from dawdling, too. You have set goals for yourself, so stick to them.

If you did not eat your peas when you were little, your mother forced you to eat a few, at the very least. Be your own parent. Taste a little writing when you think you don't want to write, and soon you will be lost in your writing world. That's what writers do.

You Do Not Have the Right to: Avoid Your Obligation to Spread Knowledge

Have you had an experience so life-changing that others will learn from you? Have you discovered a natural cure for baldness, cancer, obesity, or depression? Have you lived with a limitation or disease and learned to deal with it? Have you overcome a setback or survived a deadly situation? Have you known someone so profound that he or she deserves to be written about? Such experiences create an obligation in writers.

If you have information that will help the lives of others, you must write it. You must get the information out to the public. You do not have the right to keep it from others.

You Do Not Have the Right to: Say Harmful Things to Other Writers

Every writer started somewhere. Some began earlier than others and gleaned even more knowledge of grammar and punctuation from school. A few display an instinctive ability to write clearly and with style, while others must learn. No matter where we stepped onto the path, we are all on the same track. Although we may not cross the finish line at the same time, we have similar goals. The finish line is big enough and broad enough to accommodate every person who gives writing an honest try. No matter where we are on our path, we have a duty to help and encourage each other.

Many years ago a friend of mine endured a scare of a lifetime, when her son had a near-fatal motorcycle crash. In her effort to remain calm and stay positive, she wrote a set of poems about the experience while it took place, even though she had never written anything creative before. After her son recovered, she pursued her new interest in writing and asked me to attend a writers conference with her. We booked a room together, drove there together, and went to many of the events together. The conference featured private consultations and manuscript evaluations. In my evaluation, I received valuable comments about my manuscript. My friend met with a different evaluator, and when she walked out, tears filled her eyes. "He told me I'd never be a writer and not to quit my day job," she said between sobs.

Writing had been therapeutic for her, and I felt infuriated that anyone would dare comment harshly on something so dear to her heart and pulverize her hopes of becoming a writer. My ire was justified, because we were at a writers conference, a place where attendees paid good money to learn about writing and gain encouragement.

Writers of fiction, nonfiction, or poetry often tie their emotions and experiences into their work. Your comments must never imply that someone's life experience was less than worthy, but you can still be honest about what would improve the writing. When others ask you to evaluate their writing, view it on two levels. See the subject matter and the writing quality separately.

Subject Matter: If you comment on the subject matter, refer to the substance, not to the author. Refer to the characters, rather than the author, when appropriate, as well. For example, instead of saying, "My son had an accident, too, but I didn't fall apart like you did," you could say, "I can see that a great deal of emotion comes through in this writing."

In another case, instead of saying, "You shouldn't have left your husband when he was down," you could say, "I see that the main character left her husband in a lurch; perhaps we need to see more of the husband's point of view here."

Writing Quality: Look for ways to be helpful. Instead of telling someone to keep his day job, recommend books that he might read to improve his work. Instead of saying, "This doesn't make any sense," you could say, "This needs to be clarified for readers."

Critique the writing, but not the writer. Instead of "You could write this better if you didn't use passive voice," say, "The manuscript uses a great deal of passive voice. It would benefit from more active verbs."

You Do Not Have the Right to: Devote Energy to Your Manuscript Rejections

Rejection slips are good indicators that you are sending out your work, but they also impress negative images in our brains. Don't spend much time with rejection letters. Instead, take time to learn how to improve your next submission.

When I set a goal of selling an article to a new publisher every three months, I taped the rejection slips to my office wall as a reminder that I was submitting work regularly. A good friend spotted those papers and said, "Whoa! Is rejection what you want to see while you're trying to sell your work?"

I took down the pages and filed them away. I continued to deposit rejections in a folder that I tucked away. I learned not to agonize over rejections, and soon I was getting more acceptances.

Display positive reminders of the good things you have accomplished. Stash away the rejection slips and get on to the next submission.

You Do Not Have the Right to: Avoid Submitting Work for Fear of Rejection

"I write for myself; I don't even try to get published," one writer told me. He asked me to read his work. I did, and I agreed; he wrote for himself. He did not polish or rewrite. He did nothing to upgrade his writing or edit for style. He put words on paper and moved on to his next project. He had only himself to satisfy. Why, then, did he ask me to read what he had written? He was fooling only himself.

My journals probably qualify for that same type of writing; I never revise journal entries, because I do not intend for anyone else to read them. I would never, however, bring a journal entry to read in a critique circle or ask someone to read and evaluate it.

If you write only for yourself, don't expect others to read your writing. If you use the "I write for myself" or the "I write for my own enjoyment" statement as an excuse to avoid facing rejection, though, that's another matter.

How can you tell whether you truly write for yourself? If you refuse to rewrite, tighten, clean up his writing, or write with style, your writing faces little chance of getting published, so you may as well admit you write for yourself. If you take writing classes and seminars, read books and magazine articles on writing, and do what you can to improve your work, you want to get it published, and to do that, you must submit your work and face rejection.

Proposal, technical, and advertising copy writers do not have to go through the same formal system of submission as the creative writer, but those who write short stories, poetry, fiction, and nonfiction must submit work and face potential rejection.

Not everyone wins, but give the competition a good run for the money. Many marathon runners enter the race with completion, not winning, in mind. Think of your writing as a marathon and cross the finish line by submitting your work. Accept your rejections and file them away and resubmit your work elsewhere.

Fail to submit your work, and you'll always fail reach your goal.

You Do Not Have the Right to: Take Rejection Personally

Manuscripts are our babies; we breathe life in them and give birth to them, but we must cut the cord and see them as separate from ourselves.

In one of my critique circles years ago, we had a romance writer who had much to learn. In the critiques, members questioned minuscule details and pointed out elements that most of us already knew. After months of hearing how much she had to repair in her novel, the writer broke into tears, left the meeting, and never returned. She forgot a vital piece of information: Her fellow writers were evaluating her manuscript, not her. They were not saying, "You are a rotten person," although that's how she interpreted their comments and recommendations.

When someone offers criticism of your manuscript, do not take it personally. Consider the advice and then do as you choose.

You Do Not Have the Right to: Dull Your Senses

Creative people ride emotional roller coasters. They feel emotions more keenly than folks who lean on linear, pragmatic thinking. Instead of worrying about your emotional swings, think of them as a carnival ride. Don't flatten out the highs and level off the lows; mine them for material. Give those emotions to your characters, because you will know those feelings well.

You've probably heard quotes from creative people who claimed they wrote best while drunk or drugged, but don't fall for that trap. Addicted people find all sorts of excuses to maintain their addictions. Remember that Hemingway shot himself and stole future literature from us. Imagine how much he could have produced had he stayed sober and alive!

Drinking is not a basis for creativity and productivity. Alcohol is a depressant. If you feel sad, alcohol makes you feel worse. Other drugs hide your emotions, give you false emotions, or fool you into thinking you are being creative.

To prove the point, I will tell a story on myself. I lived through the high times, pun intended, of the 1960s. I did not seek out drugs, but all around me, peers smoked pot and handed me joints at any gathering of friends. I often passed the marijuana to the next person without partaking, but early in the hippie era I tried it myself. Stoned on pot one night, I had such a creative revelation that I sensed that I had the complete plot for my next novel. Conscious that I might forget it the next day, I found paper and pencil and wrote down the flash of brilliance that had come to me while I washed dishes in my altered state.

The next morning I awoke and dashed into the kitchen to find the paper that would lead me to write the Great American Novel. I found it. In a scrawl similar to the handwriting I used in third grade, I had written, "Uncle Hank looks like a teapot."

I stared at the paper in shock. I had reverted to the age of about nine years old, and I had thought myself creative? The incident scared me so much that I stayed away from drugs from then on. I had a cheap, early lesson for which I am thankful. I did not have to sink into dependence or depression to realize drugs led to illogical thinking and impaired creativity.

I am not contradicting myself when I recommend that chemically depressed people seek help. Chemical depression is a physical condition that may require antidepressants or other medication. If you need a prescription medicine, take it, but you do not have the right to self-medicate. America's future literature depends on you, so stay alert and write.

15

BONUS CHAPTER FOR NONFICTION WRITERS

For much of this book I've applied my theories to fiction and nonfiction, but this chapter gives you secrets to writing better nonfiction specifically. Yes, the same principles apply to fiction, but the issues I'll address in this chapter don't come up as often in fiction as they do in nonfiction, which includes creative nonfiction, reports, textbooks, and technical writing.

Slants and Yellow Journalism

As journalists, we report facts in a neutral manner and make the people we interview look their best. Ha! In truth, we all have a bit of the jaded journalist inside us. We like some interviewees better than others just as we favor certain points of view more than others. Be conscious of your prejudices before you begin, and perhaps you can better handle them to make your presentation a well-rounded one that allows readers to make up their own minds.

Sometimes, though, our article assignments come from periodicals that have a slant. Such publications might originate with a religious organization, political party, or academic institution. When that happens, you must follow the intended slant. A Catholic magazine would not represent an abortion doctor in a positive manner, for example, any more than a Democratic publication would interview a Libertarian candidate and make him look great.

Intentional slants, though, don't bother me as much as unintentional ones, sometimes created by word choice, the selection of quotations, or the wording of quotations. Get this now: We do not have to quote everyone word for word. If we want to represent our interviewee in the best light, we may sometimes delete words or add others that get the point across and make the person look good. You already know to delete repetition as well as hesitation, such as *ah, um,* and *er.* Let's look at other deletions that make you look better as a writer and make your interviewees look better, as well.

I Feel I Think I Remember That I Know What You Believe

Everyone has memories and opinions, so certain words that key those recollections or beliefs become superfluous. Look for unnecessary words in quotations and delete them. The two sets of words I delete the most when I edit interviews are *I think* and *I remember.* Look at these examples and their stronger rewrites:

"I think I was about five years old when I first became interested in singing."
Better: "I was about five when I became interested in singing."

"I remember my granny. She would always bake pies on Saturday night, so we would have them to eat on Sunday."

Better: "Granny always baked pies on Saturday night so we had them to eat on Sunday."

"The thing I remember from my first year at ABC Corporation was that I was put on a team and expected to become a part of it."
Better: "My first year at ABC Corporation, I learned how to become part of a team."

From my examples and rewrites, I hope you noticed that the tighter rewrites did not change the intent of the interviewees' statements, but it made them appear to speak in more concise, less-passive ways. No one you interview will say you misquoted him or her, if you make your interviewees speak in an even better way than they actually did.

Granted, this opinion is mine, and we're all entitled to one, but after I spent more than forty years interviewing people and writing articles, the only person who ever said I misquoted him was one I did not misquote; I just embarrassed him by quoting him correctly. That's the way of human nature. Make people look good, and you won't upset them.

Journalists don't work for the people they interview, usually, so you have to strike a happy medium and present the interviewees in the best light while you also write a good article for your publisher.

In summary, *believe* and *feel* often replace *think*. You can often ditch those words with nothing lost.

"I believe that education makes a person more open to new ideas."
Better: "Education makes people more open to new ideas."

"The way I feel, dancing is great exercise, even if you can't do it well."
Better: "Dancing is great exercise, even if you can't do it well."

"I feel like my early years were wasted before I knew what career path I wanted to take."
Better: "I wasted my early years, before I decided on my career path."

Kill These Words and Save Your Copy

Nonfiction covers much more than periodical articles. Nonfiction can also be advertising or promotional copy and copy for websites. It can also be proposals and reports and memos and white papers and sales letters. The list goes on and on. In this type of writing your mission is the reverse of journalism. You want to slant your copy in a way that makes readers respond. You want to move them to action. Again, certain words work, while others don't.

I won't try to teach you how to write persuasive copy; entire books cover that subject. What I can do in a couple of paragraphs is to give you tips that help you write in style, so that even unprofessional copy becomes more persuasive.

Here goes: Use as few words as necessary. Sounds simple, doesn't it? It's not. Let me address the deadly words you must delete.

Help!

You thought you could persuade people by telling them you help them, but most people don't want help; they want you to do the work. In your advertising copy, you might have a choice of these two mottoes: *We help make your flight easier. We make your flight easier.* Which is better? The shorter, tighter one that shows that the company does all the work for the customer. Look at these pairs and watch a pattern emerging:

WXYZ will help make your drive home more pleasant.
Better: WXYZ makes your drive home pleasant.

MarFab will help brighten your kitchen.
Better: MarFab brightens your kitchen.

Use Manco tools to help you get the job done right.
Better: Manco tools get the job done right.

Don't Try, Do!

"Do or do not; there is no try." What famous person made that statement? Fooled you; it wasn't a person, it was Yoda, in *Star Wars*.

Try, a word that appears harmless on the surface, rarely has a place in advertising copy or proposals. You would not want to read a proposal that says this: *We try to do good work.* Why? Because it implies that although you try, you may not achieve your goals. That example is blatant and would not appear in any ad copy or proposal, yet I've seen sentences like this: *We try to find the best sources at lowest prices.* Always re-write, perhaps like this: *We find the best sources at the lowest prices.*

Can, Will, and Other Auxiliary Verbs

Deleting most auxiliary verbs strengthens your advertising copy, memos, letters, and proposals, too. Auxiliary verbs include words such as these: *can, will, would, should, have,* and *had*. When you find them, they present an opportunity to write in style.

> We can make your deck look brand new.
> **Better:** We make your deck look brand new.

> We will inspect your house for insects, and if we do find any, we will exterminate them.
> **Better:** We inspect your home, and if we find insects, we exterminate them.

> We would like to be of service to you.
> **Better:** We want to be of service to you.

> You should give us a call today.
> **Better:** Call us today.

Not every auxiliary verb must go, but many trigger opportunities to polish your prose.

Find 'Em and Reap

When you want to strengthen your nonfiction writing, use the Find and Refine Method on each of the words in the list below. Every time your computer stops on one, ponder whether it is an opportunity to write tighter, stronger, more persuasive prose.

- Believe
- Can
- Could
- Feel

- Have
- Help
- Know
- Remember
- Should
- Think
- Try
- Will
- Would

Ready to Write in Style?

Below are some exercises to allow you to look for sneaky little words that could be the key to writing stronger, more persuasive nonfiction. My suggested changes follow, but your responses, as usual, may be even better than mine.

1. I can still remember that every fall, Mother went out into her garden and dug up hundreds of bulbs, and I'll never forget the whine of the old refrigerator in the garage, where she stored her bulbs.
2. He could see the sun setting on the horizon, and he heard the loons calling on the water.
3. The management feels that employees will adjust to their new positions better if they are given an orientation first.
4. Our consultants can help your business reach more potential clients.
5. When you send your managers to our training classes, they should return to you more valuable than before and they will always remember the lessons we tried to teach them.

6. When the CEO saw the numbers changing after he tried his new method, he knew he had found the solution to the financial drain of the previous year.
7. I believe you will like the revised proposal and look forward to hearing from you.
8. If you would like, we can do the work in one week.
9. Of all the lessons I learned in life, I think the most important was that people like to be treated well.
10. If you will fill in the form and return it to us, and we will start work immediately.

Here are my suggested rewrites. What are yours?

1. In the fall, Mother dug up hundreds of bulbs from her garden. She stored the dormant tubers in an old refrigerator that whined in a corner of the garage.
2. The sun set on the horizon, and the call of loons carried across the water.
3. Management knows that employees who go through an orientation adjust to their new positions better.
4. Our consultants show you how to reach more targeted prospects than ever.
5. Send your managers to our training classes, and they return more valuable than ever. Our methods ensure they put their lessons to use and never forget them.
6. The CEO applied the new methods, the numbers changed, and the financial drain of the previous year came to an end.
7. You will like the revised proposal. I look forward to hearing from you.

8. We perform the work in one week.

9. The most important lesson I learned in life is that people like to be treated well.

10. Fill in the form and return it to us, and we start work immediately.

CHARACTER TRAIT CHART

Make copies of this character trait chart and fill one out for each of your main fiction characters. Some writers add a photo of a real person or a picture from a magazine that allows them to visualize their character.

Name_____

Alias(es) _____

Age_____

Birth date _____

Height _____

Weight_____

Sex _____

Birthplace_____

Hair color _____

Eye color_____

Scars, tattoos, birthmarks, etc.

_____

Handicaps and/or flaws

_____

Habits

_____

Education

_____

Work experience

_____

Significant other, best friend, other friends

_____

Enemies

_____

Why are they enemies?

_____

Parents' names & traits

_____

Current problem/conflict/desire (What does this character want?)

_____

How does problem/conflict/desire worsen and/or who gets in the way?

_____

How is problem/conflict/desire resolved?

_____

Strongest trait

_____

Weakest trait

_____

How person sees self

_____

How others see person

_____

What makes this person laugh?

_____

Basic nature

_____

Ambitions

_____

Philosophy/Religion

_____

Hobbies

_____

Preferred music

_____

Dialogue style

_____

Interests

_____

Style of dress

_____

Favorite colors

_____

Atmosphere of home (physical, mental, emotional)

_____

Most important thing about person

_____

One-line characterization

_____

What trait makes character come alive?

_____

Why is this person worth writing about?

_____

What emotional baggage is character carrying?

_____

How is person different from similar characters?

_____

Do I like or dislike this person and why?

_____

Will readers like or dislike this person for same reasons?

_____

What's this character's weak spot?

_____

Who finds his/her weak spot?

_____

What does that character do with the information?

_____

Which character does this character care most about?

_____

TIPS AND TERMINOLOGY

The information below is intentionally brief. Some items are covered in more detail elsewhere in this book; others can be found in other resources.

Acronym

Acronyms are words formed from initials, such as scuba (self-contained underwater breathing apparatus), radar (radio detecting and ranging), WAC (Women's Army Corps), or AIDS (acquired immune deficiency syndrome). Not all abbreviations are acronyms. IBM, EPA, LSD, etc., are initials pronounced as letters, so they are not acronyms. If it cannot be pronounced as a word—if it has to be enunciated as letters—it is not an acronym.

Adjective

A word used to modify a noun. Adjectives usually precede the noun they modify, and adjectives limit, qualify, describe, or specify the noun. In the case of the following sentence, the adjectives include *brilliant* and *afternoon*: *Brilliant flowers swayed in the afternoon breeze.*

Be careful not to string adjectives together, as in this sentence: *The large, tall purple flowers swayed in the light, cool afternoon breeze.* One adjective is better than two or more, because the effect gets reduced with each additional adjective.

Adverb

Words that can modify verbs, adjectives, and other adverbs. Careful writers consider an adverb an opportunity to find a more powerful verb. For example, instead of writing *He walked slowly,* choose *He sauntered.* Instead of *Jane quickly jumped onto the table,* choose *Jane leaped onto the table.*

Ambiguity

Ambiguity is a word, phrase, or statement that contains more than one meaning. When words have more than one meaning, they can cause uncertainty in readers. To avoid confusion, careful writers choose words that are clear in context and place them in an order that is clear to readers. In the following example, the character appears to have a head full of eyebrows and hair: *He had a full head of snow-white hair and bushy gray eyebrows.* To avoid the ambiguity, recast the sentence this way: *He had bushy gray eyebrows and a full head of snow-white hair.* Nouns that can also be verbs can result in ambiguity, as in the following examples: *Protesters rock the capital.* (Did they throw rocks or simply cause a disturbance?) *He boxed her.* (Did he hit her or put her in a box?)

Antagonist

Sometimes "the bad guy" in a work of fiction, but the antagonist is the character who stands in the way of allowing the protagonist to get what he or she wants.

Apostrophe (and Apostrophes Turned Wrong)

An apostrophe is a mark used to indicate the omission of letters or figures, the possessive case, or the plural of letters or figures. Apostrophes always turn in only one direction; if turned in the other direction, they become single quotation marks. When using smart or curly quotes, a correct apostrophe starts at the top with the fattest part, rounds to the right, and points left at the bottom. (') Conversely, an opening single quotation mark (') turns the opposite way. It starts at the top with a point, rounds to the left, and ends with the largest portion at the bottom. Unfortunately both marks are formed with a single key on the computer, the key that in the uppercase mode is a double quotation mark ("). Computer programs that create curly quotes sometimes therefore turn apostrophes the wrong way, making them single quotation marks. This mistake happens often when an author attempts to write dialect, using apostrophes where they do not ordinarily appear, for example at the beginning of a word, such as *'em*.

Attribution

Sometimes called tags, attribution refers to words that connect a quotation to a specific person. Examples: *He said, Rachel remarked, Josh answered, Laura replied, Joe repeated, Lycia asked.*

Auxiliary Verb

A verb such as *have, had, can, could, will,* or *would* that accompanies the main verb in a clause and helps make distinctions in mood, voice, aspect, and tense. One use of the auxiliary verb per scene is usually enough to set the tense.

Book Doctor

An independent editor who evaluates and edits manuscripts and gives advice to writers. Editors who worked at publishing houses once performed this service, but few publishers provide the service anymore. Many publishers expect authors to hire a qualified book doctor to polish their manuscripts.

Book Proposal

A book proposal is a business proposition that outlines a nonfiction book and sets forth specific and required information, such as subject matter, market, qualifications of the writers, competition, and the author's plans to promote the book. With a good book proposal, writers can potentially sell a nonfiction book before finishing writing it. A mediocre or incomplete proposal is a waste of a writer's time, so be sure to follow a good book on how to write a proposal and do not leave out any sections. Especially complete the research on the market for your book and quantify all statistics, rather than using vague terms such as "This book will appeal to everyone."

Chapter-by-Chapter Outline
See **Outline**

Characters

Characters are the people in a work of fiction or nonfiction. Careful writers pay close attention to their characters and get to know them intimately, to ensure their dialogue and actions portray the characters accurately and consistently. Main characters are those who have large and important roles in the plot. Authors should not give minor characters—peripheral characters—the same amount of description or attention as main characters. Many minor characters do not even need to be named, but can be referred in ways such as the bus driver, the doctor, the professor, the woman in blue, the dimpled man, the little girl, the one with the deep voice, and such.

Character Development

As the story progresses, the main characters should grow in depth with the readers through their actions and dialogue more than through narrative that tells, rather than shows. By the end of the story the main character should shift in some way, either for the better or for the worse, because of having undergone the setbacks or successes reflected in the plot.

Character Flaw

The best novels have main characters that are in some way flawed. Perfect people rarely occur in real life, and in fiction, perfect characters do not hold readers' interest. The flaw can be physical, such as an ailment or disability, or mental, such as having anger issues or post-traumatic stress syndrome. The character flaw can be an addiction, such as gambling or alcohol, or any number of other possibilities.

Chicago Style

Chicago style refers to the recommendations set out in *The Chicago Manual of Style*, published by the University of Chicago Press. The book in its sixteenth edition at the writing of this book has more than a thousand pages. Chicago style sets the standards for the book publishing industry when it comes to such things as punctuation, capitalization, and when to spell out a numeral or use the Arabic number.

Cliché

A cliché is any idiom or saying you have heard before, such as *cute as a button, quiet as a mouse, smart like a fox, scared to death, tried and true, avoid it like the plague, skeletons in the closet,* and *talk up a blue streak.* Sometimes clichés are sets of words used often together, such as *abject terror, mischievous grin, sordid past,* and *death rattle.* Avoid using clichés in narrative. Let the urge to use a cliché signal an opportunity to write something more creative or informative. Clichés in dialogue are acceptable in moderation, because people often speak in overused, worn-out phrases.

Climax

A story climaxes when the situation becomes almost too impossible for the protagonist to handle, and everything comes to a head. In novels, the climax takes place at or near the end of the story, as a rule.

Conflict

To be marketable, novels usually must be based on conflict—a main character who wants to get or achieve something and the people or things that impede the wishes of the main character. Without conflict, a story becomes a saga, which many readers and publishers consider a less compelling tale.

Content or Concept Editing

Content editing or concept editing refers to editing of the broader aspects of a manuscript, such as plot development or character development. It does not include line editing.

Conjunction

A part of speech such as *and, but, as, or,* and *nor* that serves to connect words, phrases, clauses, or sentences. Avoid using conjunctions at the beginning of a sentence, because it creates a sentence fragment.

Copyright

The exclusive legal right to reproduce, publish, sell, or distribute the matter and form of intellectual property, including books, short stories, or poems. Upon completion of such work, the person who produces it automatically owns the copyright to that work, according to the law, so the only time the copyright needs to be formally registered with the U.S. Copyright Office is when the work is polished and ready to go to print without a single additional change. See www.copyright.gov.

Cover Letter

The cover letter accompanies and introduces a manuscript. A well-written, business-like cover letter entices the receiver to read more. Also see **Query Letter**.

Creative Nonfiction

Real-life stories written in an entertaining style that captures the imagination of readers. The true stories in collections such as *Chicken Soup for the Soul* and the *Cup of Comfort* series or in *Readers Digest* and *Guideposts* magazines, for example, are creative nonfiction. Creative nonfiction often evokes emotion or inspiration in the reader and employs action, dialogue, and conflict, which makes it read like fiction.

Crescendo

Although misused enough to become acceptable English to some, *crescendo* does not mean *climax*. It means to build slowly in intensity. Purists prefer not to see *crescendo* used to mean *climax*. If insistent upon using *crescendo* to mean *climax*, remember one cannot *build to a crescendo,* which is redundant.

Dangling Modifier

Modifying—or descriptive—phrases must have logical relationships to some specific words in the sentence. When those words are omitted, the phrase "dangles" without anything to modify. Dangling modifiers frequently occur at the beginnings of sentences. Correct them by adding the proper subjects (nouns or pronouns) to the main clauses. Examples: Dangling—*Not knowing how to swim, buying scuba gear was foolish.* Correct—*Not knowing how to swim, we decided that buying scuba gear was foolish.* Even better: *We did not know how to swim, so we decided that buying scuba gear was foolish.*

Dangling Participle

The same as the above, dangling modifier, except that it always involves an "ing" word. Example: *Laughing at the rain, our umbrellas caught the wind and inverted.* Correct: *While we laughed at the rain, our umbrellas caught the wind and inverted.*

Denouement (day-noo-MA)

The denouement comes after the climax, when the protagonist overcomes the obstacles and reverses the situation. It can also be called *resolution.*

Dialect

A variety of dialogue distinguished by pronunciation, grammar, or vocabulary. Cockney is a dialect of British English, for example. Although characters each should have a distinct style of speaking, dialect that relies on misspellings or missing letters is difficult to write, hard to maintain, and difficult to understand. Here are examples of poor dialect: *She cum walzin' frum Alibammy with a banjer on her nee*. Here are the problems with that method of dialect: 1. Never misspell something in dialect that would be pronounced the same, even if spelled correctly. *Cum*, *frum*, and *nee* are all pronounced the same, no matter how they are spelled, so spell them correctly. 2. Continued odd spellings and dropped letters such as *walzin'*, *Alibammy*, and *banjer* slow comprehension. When readers must reread a sentence to understand it, they realize they are reading. You lose them for the moment. Never lose your reader. To indicate that a character speaks in dialect, use dialect in an opening phrase or sentence, lightly sprinkle a single word or two of dialect throughout his or her speech, and the reader gets the message without having to continue to plow through odd words, misspellings, foreign phrases, and such. Another good way to indicate dialect is to show it outside the dialogue, such as this example: *"I saw your mother." She pronounced it sar*. The most common show of dialect appears when authors leave off the last letter—especially with "ing"—and use an apostrophe to show the missing letter: I *was laughin'. What were you sayin'?* Because of the overuse of this formation, it has become a cliché and adds little to nothing to the dialect, except to slow readers down. Avoid dropping the *g* in "ing" words.

Dialogue

Conversation with two or more people. Internal dialogue reflects internal conversations with oneself. Internal dialogue and thoughts are often the same thing. While a good work of fiction should be about seventy percent dialogue, good writers do not let their characters speak too many sentences in a row without a break, lest the dialogue turn into a monologue.

Editor

At a publishing house, almost everyone has the title of editor, but few edit, anymore. When agents use the term "editor," they usually mean an acquisitions editor, the one who makes the initial offer for a manuscript. Magazine publishers and book publishers also may have managing editors and business editors, as well, but they usually handle business affairs, rather than editing.

Electronic Editing

The term is a misnomer, because it implies that an electronic device does the editing, whereas in truth a human being performs the edit; however, the human edits the electronic file, rather than the printed version of the manuscript. Most editors who work on electronic files use Track Changes, a function available in Microsoft Word. Also see **Track Changes**.

Elements of Fiction

The main elements of fiction include plot, setting, character(s), conflict, symbol, and point of view. Theme, if there is one, can also be an element. A good evaluation covers all these elements plus addresses anything that would make a manuscript even stronger.

Exclamation/Interjection

An exclamation or interjection is an abrupt, forceful utterance or outcry that expresses emotion. Exclamations or interjections usually stand alone and are followed by an exclamation point. Examples: *Ugh! Wow! Crap!* Also see **Exclamation Point/Exclamation Mark**.

Exclamation Point/Exclamation Mark

A punctuation mark that follows an exclamatory statement, as in *Look!* or *Holy cow!* Do not use exclamation points to make sentences sound powerful. Reserve them for their proper use. Incorrect: *"Only two boys are left in the race!"* Correct: *"Wow! Only two boys are left in the race."*

Exposition

A discourse that exposes information about or an explanation of difficult or background material. It always tells, rather than shows.

Fiction

Stories created out of the imagination, such as short stories and novels. While fiction can be based loosely on truth, it expands on the truth and involves creative development of a story. All novels are fiction, by the way, so to call a novel a fictionalized novel, a fiction novel, or a novel of fiction is redundant.

Fifty-Cent Word

While members of my former critique circle recommended that I adjust this term for inflation and call it a fifty-dollar word, the term *fifty-cent word* still refers to a word that is longer and more elevated than its synonym. For example, *ebullition* is a fifty-cent word that means *boiling*. Most people know what *boiling* means, but few will understand *ebullition*, so stick to the smaller, better-known word, boiling. *Hirsute* is another word that comes to mind as a fifty-cent word. People understand *hairy*, but will they understand *hirsute*?

Find Function

Most computers have a Find function. The Find function allows you to type in words or letters, and the computer searches the manuscript, finds the next use (or all the uses) of those words or letters, and allows you to make changes, if you wish. The Find and Refine Method employs the Find function to help writers be objective about their work and find more "missed opportunities for improvement" than they would on their own.

Find and Refine Method

The Find and Refine Method is a technique I created to make manuscript revision easier. With it writers use the Find function on their computer to locate and then revise specific words and phrases that have been either misused or overused.

Flashback

An interjected scene that relates events or situations that occurred before the current scene. Flashbacks should relate relevant information through action and dialogue, rather than narrative, and should give insight into the plot or the character and his or her motivations. After a flashback, always provide a clear transition back to the present.

Genre

A category marked by a distinctive style, form, or content. Genre fiction includes romance, science fiction, mystery, psychological thriller, mainstream, and so forth.

Gerund

A noun derived from a verb, often by adding "ing." Strong writers do their best to shun the use of gerunds and instead choose the active form of the verb. Examples: *The choir began singing. Elephants were parading through the tent.* Better: *The choir sang. Elephants paraded through the tent.* The overuse of "ing" words reduces the power of the prose.

Hard Copy

The printed form of a manuscript. Before the advent of computers and the Internet, all editing and submissions were handled by hard copy. Writers mailed manuscripts to editors, agents, or publishers. Today most submissions to editors, agents, and publishers are electronic, sent over the Internet. As a result, few submissions are handled in hard copy anymore, although some agents and publishers do still request hard copies. Before submitting to agents or publishers, research their preferences and submit accordingly.

Hard-Copy Editing

Hard-copy editing refers to a process whereby a client prints out a manuscript and ships it to an independent editor for editing. The editor then uses a distinctive color of ink or a pencil to mark the manuscript to indicate where the author needs to make changes to the content, grammar, punctuation, capitalization, and spelling. When I perform a hard-copy edit,

I use bright red ink, so clients can see each change clearly. I also include a written evaluation that evaluates the elements of the story, explains my recommended changes, and may make other suggestions for improvement. Hard-copy editing used to be the standard in the industry; however, nowadays much more work is performed on the electronic file, rather than on a printed copy.

Homonym

Words that sound alike but differ in meaning. Homonyms can lead to errors in manuscripts, as in the following case: *The nurse carried a vile of blood. Vile* and *vial* are pronounced the same, but have different meanings. In some cases, as in this one, the error can strike a reader as funny, because it makes sense in a humorous way. In hard-copy editing, editors write "W. C." or "word choice" beside words that are close or are homonyms but are not the right choice, as in the following example: *Her breasts peaked out above her blouse.* The correct word choice, or homonym, is *peeked*. While on the subject of *peak* and *peek*, let me add that *pique* is often meant, when *peak* or *peek* is used, as in this case: *Your story peaked my interest.* The correct word is *piqued. Your story piqued my interest.*

Hook

The sentence or paragraph that promises a reader something interesting and makes the reader want to read more. The hook is best when placed at the beginning of a book, article, story, or chapter.

Hybrid Editing

I created the term *hybrid editing* because it combines some of the elements of hard-copy editing with electronic editing. Hybrid editing includes a complete line edit plus a written evaluation of the elements of the manuscript.

Internal Dialogue

Thoughts not expressed verbally. Writers can write thoughts in quotation marks, italics, or regular type, as long as thoughts are handled consistently throughout the manuscript. Thoughts tell, rather than show, whereas regular dialogue shows, rather than tells. Showing is better than telling, so take a moment to ponder all instances of internal dialogue or thoughts. Consider writing them into dialogue in a conversation with another character.

Line Edit

A line edit corrects things that are technically wrong in a manuscript, such as grammar, punctuation, capitalization, and syntax. A line edit does not address the bigger picture, such as plot, pacing, and characterization.

Mainstream Fiction

Fiction for general audiences; what most people buy, as opposed to specific genres, such as romance, mystery, adventure, science fiction, fantasy, and so forth. Mainstream fiction is considered a genre in itself, but is broader in scope than most genres and can include other genres.

Manuscript

A neatly typed version of an article, book, or poetry collection that follows standard manuscript format. Also see

Standard Manuscript Format. Whereas a manuscript used to be a printed version, today manuscripts can also be electronic files.

Misplaced Modifier

When modifying words, phrases, or clauses are not near the word they describe, confusion or unintentional humor often results. Example, misplaced: *I watched the sun as it set below the horizon and wished for a margarita.* As written, the sun wanted the drink. Correct: *I wished for a margarita while I watched the sun set below the horizon.*

Monologue

Dialogue spoken by one person. Can also be internal dialogue. Long monologues, also called soliloquies, might have been fine in Shakespeare's day, but they are not recommended in contemporary fiction. Good writers avoid using more than two sentences in a row without a break for action, attribution, or reaction by another character.

Narrative

The narrative portion of a manuscript is anything that is not in dialogue. Background information and descriptions of characters and settings usually come out in narrative form. Writers of fiction should strive for a balance of 70% dialogue to only 30% narrative.

Nonfiction

Any prose that sticks to the facts. Nonfiction books may be called books, whereas novels are called fiction. Magazine, newsletter, or newspaper articles; interviews; business writing;

brochure copy; reports; web copy; advertising; and white papers are forms on nonfiction. How-to books, reference books, textbooks, essays, editorials, memoirs, biographies, autobiographies, and personal experiences are also nonfiction. Also see **Creative Nonfiction.**

Noun

A person, place, or thing. Nouns can be concrete, as in the words *bench, tree, mouse, house, hair, dog,* or *chair.* They can be abstract, as in the words *autumn, happiness, horticulture, health, livelihood,* or *shame.* The names of people, places, or things are capitalized and called proper nouns. Here are a few proper nouns: *Washington, Europe, Elm Street, Smithsonian Institute, Mt. Sinai Hospital,* and *John Hancock.* The names of courses, such as *geology, history,* and *biology* are not capitalized, because they are not proper nouns; however, *English, Spanish, French,* and other language courses are capitalized, because languages are capitalized. The names of things such as plants and animal breeds are not capitalized unless they include a proper noun; hence we have *German shepherd, Chihuahua, poodle, elm, daisies,* and *Bradford pear.*

Nuance

A subtle shade of meaning, as in the difference between the words *stride* and *stomp.* One implies a more aggressive style of walking than the other. Whenever considering a choice among words, decide which choice you prefer based on the nuance, the tone of the word.

Outline

A summary of a written work, usually depicted in headings and subheadings. It can be either the preliminary draft for the author or it can be a complete outline written for the benefit of agents and publishers. A chapter-by-chapter outline gives the chapter numbers and/or titles and a few sentences that describe what takes place in each chapter.

Oxford Comma

See **Serial Comma**

Pace

Pace refers to the speed at which a novel or short story moves. If the pace is too slow, readers grow disinterested. If the pace is too fast, readers get exhausted and may get disoriented. Good pacing is a balance between quick scenes filled with action and dialogue and slower scenes and narrative passages. Short sentences with action verbs pick up the pace, as can dialogue. Long sentences and monologues slow down the pace. Good writers strive for a balance in the pace that moves the story forward and keeps readers interested without wearing them out.

Participle

A form of a verb that can function independently as an adjective. In the following example, *baked* is a participle: *The baked pie lay on the table.* In this example, *dancing* is a participle: *The dancing bear brought many children to the circus.* Also see **Dangling Modifiers**, which are sometimes **Dangling Participles**.

Passive Income

Income derived from sources that require no extra work. Books, for example, can provide passive income for authors who, upon completion of the book, continue to sell it many times.

Plot

Plot is the main story of a work of fiction and usually involves conflict or desire. To describe the plot, describe what the protagonist (the central character) wants and what conflicts and setbacks he or she must attempt to overcome. In strong plots, the protagonists try to surmount the conflicts and achieve what they want but get into deeper trouble, usually from the antagonists, the people who stand in the way. The story climaxes when the situation becomes almost too impossible to handle, and the denouement comes when the protagonist overcomes the obstacles and reverses the situation or gives up.

Point of View (also called Viewpoint)

The way the author of a novel allows readers to "see" and "hear" what's going on. Point of view shows readers the opinion, emotional reactions, or feelings of the individuals involved in a situation. Point of view can be through the main character in each scene or omniscient and all-knowing. An omniscient point of view can report everything that takes place in a novel, but a point of view in third person though the main character in the scene can show only what that character sees, hears, and knows. Contemporary novels should follow the guidelines for point of view, but point of view is a complex issue that cannot be explained fully in a short note. Writers unfamiliar with point of view should read books and attend seminars that teach how to handle point of view correctly.

Proofreading

The final read before a book goes to a printer. Proofreading takes place after a book has been written, edited, and designed for layout, and it does not replace editing, because editing is much more thorough and intense than proofing. Every change to a manuscript includes the risk of making an error, so proofreading catches the final small glitches and layout flaws that crept in during the final edit and layout.

Prose

Speech or writing that is not poetry.

Protagonist

The main character, usually the good guy in a story—the one who wants something.

Pseudonym

Also can be called a pen name, alias, or a nom de plume, a pseudonym is a fictitious name the author uses to conceal his or her identity. Authors may choose to use a pseudonym for any number of reasons. Some authors use a different name for each genre in which they write.

Purple Prose

Overwriting that is often combined with far-fetched ideas and is usually a failed attempt to write poetic prose. Here are two real-life examples of purple prose ripped from raw manuscripts: *The autobiography drips with famous names that roll off the tongue like bacon grease sliding down the slippery sunny-side-up slope of a fried egg. His reaction made the bare bones truth a walking, breathing dragon that burned a hole in their friendship.* [See chapter three for the classic purple prose of Bulwer-Lytton.]

Query Letter

A query letter is an attempt to entice a publisher to request a short story, magazine article, or book-length manuscript. A well-written query letter sticks to the basics, is professional, and gives enough information to allow the publisher to make a decision whether to request the full manuscript. Query letters for nonfiction books usually should be accompanied by a book proposal.

Repetition

Writers can intentionally repeat a sound, word, or pattern as an interesting literary tactic; however, unintentional repetition reflects poorly on writers. Unfortunately I often see certain words overused in manuscripts I edit, and many times those words can be eliminated without any harm to the sentences in which they appear. Use the Find and Refine Method to see if you have overused any of the following words in your manuscript: *now, as, really, real, very, so, that, just, there were, there was, it was, began, started, suddenly,* and *well.* To ensure your computer picks up only on the words I listed and not on all the words that have those same letters in them, hit the space bar before and after typing in the word in the Find window.

SASE

Sometimes pronounced "sassy," but more often pronounced as letters, an SASE stands for self-addressed, stamped envelope. Before the Internet became the standard way to submit manuscripts, writers had to print their manuscripts and mail them, being sure always to include a SASE. Nowadays few agents and publishers demand printed submissions, but if they do, remember the following information: your SASE does not have to be large enough to return all your materials, if you prefer not to pay the additional return postage, but do send at least a #10 business-size self-addressed envelope with the current first-class postage attached. If you use a postage meter, comply with postal regulations: turn off the date stamp on the return postage, because you cannot predict when the agent or publisher will put your SASE back in the mail to you. Many agents and publishers who request printed submissions and receive them without an SASE do not respond, if they are not interested, so including a SASE may net you some valuable comments. Believe me, it's worth the trouble and cost to include a SASE with every hard-copy submission to agents and publishers.

Serial Comma

Also called an Oxford Comma, a serial comma is a comma placed immediately before the coordinating conjunction (usually *and*, *or*, or *nor*) in a series of three or more terms. AP style, which many newspapers follow, does not use the serial comma. Book publishers, however, follow Chicago style, which does call for the serial comma.

Sidebar

A short news story accompanying a major story that presents sidelights of that story. In a travel magazine, for example, a sidebar may list recommended hotels or restaurants in the locations mentioned in the main article.

Standard Manuscript Format

When submitting fiction or nonfiction, writers should submit the document in standard manuscript format. Standard format varies a little for articles, books, and short stories, so consult a comprehensive source for details. In brief, manuscripts should be double-spaced, average about 250 words a page, have margins of at least an inch on all sides, and be typed with a Courier 12-point font. Some publishers accept Times or Times New Roman, but all accept Courier. The lines should be flush left, ragged right (not justified), with about a five-space indent at the start of each paragraph. Space only once after periods; the two-space rule applied when we used typewriters, but it does not apply to computer-generated manuscripts.

Suffix

Letters added to the end of a word. In the words *laughing*, *hopelessly*, and *dancer*, the suffixes are "ing," "ly," and "er."

Synonym

A word that has the same or nearly the same meaning as another word or other words. To avoid unintentional repetition, good writers look for synonyms, rather than repeat the same word too often. For example, synonyms for *walk* include *amble*, *stroll*, *saunter*, *march*, and so forth. Before choosing a synonym, always be sure your choice has the correct nuance.

Synopsis

The synopsis, a one- or two-page single-spaced summary of a novel, is a test of the strength, plausibility, and marketability of the plot. Contrary to what many beginners think, the synopsis should not tickle the interest of a reader the way the summary, cover letter, or dust-cover copy might. A synopsis is a formal telling, in present tense, of the entire plot of the story, for the benefit of an agent or a publisher. It should not leave anyone guessing; it must tell the conclusion, including the resolution. Authors may whine that synopses do not give the effect of the great writing that goes into the book. Although the complaint is valid, agents and publishers are aware of the limitations of synopses. Unless the synopsis has errors in grammar, punctuation, or syntax, agents and publishers do not judge the quality of manuscript based on the synopsis; they judge only the plot. Instead of relying on the synopsis, agents and publishers judge the quality of the manuscript based on sample chapters of the actual manuscript or the entire manuscript. The synopsis need not reflect creative style and should never include hype, such as "This book is the next bestseller," or "The story ends with a twist." Do not include dialogue, and do not put character names in all caps, a style used in scripts for plays and movies. Do tell the whole story and the ending in the synopsis. A good synopsis gives readers enough information to decide if the subject matter is interesting, timely, and marketable.

Style

Style has two meanings.

1. The way a writer puts words together, as in word choice and creativity
2. A publisher's preferred rules for punctuation, capitalization, abbreviation, etc., as in Associated Press, academic, business, or Chicago style.

Syntax

Sentence structure, word choice, word order, and the relationship between words and other structural elements in phrases and sentences. Syntax is a better way to show ethnic origins than is dialect. For example, a person from Mexico might say in English, "He no like my work, so he fire me." If an editor says a manuscript has syntactical flaws, the author may have incorporated dangling modifiers, incorrect word choices, confusing juxtapositions, or unclear and incorrect pronouns.

Thesaurus

A reference book that lists multiple synonyms. Writers may use a thesaurus to trigger their memories for alternative words when they want to avoid repeating the same word, but they should never choose a word they have never spoken, or it marks the writing as unnatural. Not every choice is a perfect substitute for every other word listed as a synonym. Each word has its own nuance. Pick the fitting word. Consider all choices, as in this potential setup: *A pair (couple, twosome, team) of birds (chicks, vultures, pigeons, doves, ducks, hawks) flew (sailed, glided, floated, drifted, swept, soared) out of the mist (fog, haze, smog, soup).* Each word choice changes the image slightly.

Track Changes

Microsoft Word, which has become the standard software for manuscripts, has a function called Track Changes. People who edit electronic files can turn on the Track Changes function, and every change made to the file will appear in a color other than black. Track Changes also places a vertical line on the left side of any line that has been changed. Writers clearly see what has been changed and can then put their cursor on the change and right click to accept or reject each change. Track Changes also allows editors to add comments to the file that are not part of the manuscript itself. An example of such a comment might be that a name was spelled inconsistently in the manuscript, and the author has to decide which spelling to use. Because most manuscripts are edited in electronic form today, serious writers must familiarize themselves with Track Changes. The process is simple, and most people quickly catch on to how to use it.

Verb

The part of speech that expresses existence, action, or occurrence in most languages. It modifies the subject of a sentence. In the sentence *John read the book, read* (the action) is the verb, *John* is the subject (who did the action), and *book* is the object (what was read).

Voice

An identifiable way of speaking. Voice is a difficult concept for new writers to grasp, but think of some of the famous writers who had distinctive voices in their works, such as Hemingway, Dickens, and Steinbeck. Word choice and syntax dictate voice. The writer can have a voice in the narrative or a character can be the narrator in a distinctive voice. Each main character should also have a separate, distinctive voice in dialogue, often reflected in word choice, cadence, and syntax. If one character comes from New Jersey, he or she should have a voice that is different from a character reared in New Orleans. Avoid using dialect to depict voice. (See **Dialect**) When a character is the narrator of a work of fiction or nonfiction, narrative can take on a sense of dialogue. In J. D.

Salinger's *The Catcher in the Rye*, a teenage Holden Caulfield narrates the book. Here's an example of his voice in the narrative of that book: "I wasn't supposed to come back after Christmas vacation, on account of I was flunking four subjects and not applying myself and all." Notice how word choices create the character's voice.

Word Choice

Word choice in dialogue: Characters can be differentiated by their choices of words in dialogue. An uneducated character may use substandard words such as *ain't* and slur words together, such as *gonna*, for example. In contrast, a college professor might speak in stilted language and even sprinkle her dialogue with British terms such as *amongst*, instead of *among*.

Word choice in narrative: Word choice can also refer to incorrect choices in narrative, such as using *passed* when *past* is the proper choice for a specific sentence. Also see **Homonym.**

White Paper

A white paper is a detailed and authoritative report on a subject, often slanted for a specific purpose, such as to persuade customers to buy a certain product or service.

Writing on Spec

Writing on the speculation and hope that something will sell. With the rare exception of when an author has signed a multiple-book deal, in essence fiction writers write everything on spec. Nonfiction writers, however, do not always have to write on spec. If they are writing books, they can create a book proposal with a couple of sample chapters and use the proposal to find a buyer. If a publisher buys the idea, the nonfiction writer then writes the book to the specifications of the contract. Sometimes nonfiction writers produce magazine articles on spec and send completed articles to a magazine or magazines in hopes of selling the article. Many professional writers spurn the concept of writing on spec, because they must make a living writing and cannot spend time writing something in hopes that it will sell. For that reason, you may hear writers pooh-pooh writing on spec, but many successful writers spent time writing on spec before they became established in their field. Occasionally I get a request to ghostwrite or to edit a book on spec; that is, I supposedly would get paid from the proceeds of the sale, rather than getting paid up front. Because my time is all I have to sell, I cannot spend it ghostwriting and editing on spec. If I edited on spec for an individual, I would have no way of knowing the sales figures if the book did sell, so the few times I have made such arrangements, they have always been through a literary agent or publisher.

ACKNOWLEDGMENTS

Ahmad Meradji, CEO of BookLogix, if not for you and your staff, this book never would have been re-released. Ahmad, your encouragement, enthusiasm, and generosity made this second edition of *Write In Style* possible. Thank you.

Special thanks, too, to all my friends, supporters, clients, members of The Writers Network, and other fellow writers who encouraged me to re-release this book after my original publisher sold the last copy and took it out of print. Your names are far too many for me to list here, but you know who you are, and best of all, I do too.

Always and forever, posthumous thanks to my father, Michael M. Rothberg, entrepreneur, writer, terse editor in his own right, and one of my biggest supporters. I was a teen when I revealed to him that I wanted to be a writer, and his response was to give me three books: *The Elements of Style* (Strunk and White), *On Writing Well* (William Zinsser), and *Roget's International Thesaurus*, all of which I still have, ragged and overused as those books may be. He and I worked together in his business for a while, and we made a good pair. I could spell, and he could slice, dice, cut, chop, and shorten. A master at writing tight, if he were here today, he would have cut the book by hundreds of words. His challenges still surge me forward.

Speaking of books and supporters, my son Sandy was barely a teenager when we saw the movie *Roxanne*, an adaptation of the play *Cyrano de Bergerac*. In one scene in the movie, the character that Steve Martin plays is writing a love letter, and on his desk is a copy of *The Chicago Manual of Style*. I leaned over to my young son and commented, "See that book? That means he's a serious writer." For my next birthday, my son surprised me with my first copy of *The Chicago Manual of Style*. Since then the book has gone through several more editions, but I always think of my supportive son whenever I research anything in my latest copy.

SPECIAL INVITATION

The Writers Network
No rules; just write!

Free! The Writers Network is a worldwide group of all types of writers and editors—beginners, professionals, freelancers working with fiction, nonfiction, poetry, and screenplays. Members get a free subscription to *The Writers Network News*, a monthly e-zine full of information, tips, techniques, contests, resources, websites, questions and answers, events, and more of interest to writers and editors. To join go to **www.ZebraEditor.com** and click on Free Newsletter.

The Writers Network sponsor:
Zebra Communications
230 Deerchase Drive
Woodstock, GA 30188
770/924-0528
www.ZebraEditor.com

ABOUT THE AUTHOR

Bobbie Christmas owns Zebra Communications, a literary services firm in metro Atlanta that specializes in editing books for publishers and individuals.

Bobbie also produces a free monthly newsletter for writers called *The Writers Network News*. She writes a column called "Ask The Book Doctor" that appears in about two dozen websites and periodicals for writers.

Bobbie showed an interest in writing from an early age. By the early 1970s, she decided to make her living with words. Her motto became "I'll write anything for money." Since that time she has written and edited newspaper, magazine, and newsletter articles as well as press releases, brochure copy, radio commercials, advertising copy, marketing plans, children's books, and just about everything else. She managed the Corporate Communications Department for a Fortune 500 company in the 1990s before she leaped from the corporate ladder and founded Zebra Communications in 1992.

Her writing has garnered her more than a dozen awards and honors. The first edition of *Write In Style* earned three honors alone, including a Georgia Author of the Year Award and a Royal Palm Literary Award.

She has edited scores of books that clients sold to publishers or self-published. Many more are still in the revision stage.

A past president of Georgia Writers, she sat on its advisory board for more than ten years. She also is a past vice president of the South Carolina Writers Workshop and a charter lifetime member of The Florida Writers Association and coordinator of its Editors Helping Writers service.

Her home-based office provides her a perfect writing and editing space. From there she faces a huge picture window that features an ever-changing scene of birds, squirrels, chipmunks, butterflies, bushes, trees, and even the occasional rabbit. Her writing partner for the first edition of *Write In Style* was Circe the Scottish terrier, who assisted by keeping Bobbie's feet warm and by reminding her to take breaks, stretch, and play. Circe is now waiting for Bobbie in heaven, and Bobbie's current writing partner, Doodle the poodle, prefers to sleep nearby while Bobbie does all the work. He still tells her when it's time to take a break or go for a walk, though; otherwise she might sit at her computer all day and night.

Bobbie is known for her helpful advice to writers, and she welcomes questions about writing and editing. If you have a question, send it to Bobbie at Bobbie@ZebraEditor.com.

INDEX